Olav H. Hauge

Luminous Spaces

Selected Poems & Journals

Translated by Olav Grinde

WHITE PINE PRESS / BUFFALO, NEW YORK

White Pine Press
P.O. Box 236 Buffalo, NY 14201
www.whitepine.org

Publication of this book was made possible, in part, by public funds from the New York State Council on the Arts, a State Agency; with funds from the National Endowment for the Arts, which believes that a great nation deserves great art; and with the financial support of NORLA, which aims to promote the translation of Norwegian literature.

Library of Congress Control Number: 2015943682

ISBN: 978-1-935210-83-2

Overleaf: Rossvoll Farm in winter, 1954, where Hauge lived from 1937 until his death fifty-seven years later. The fertile soil has been farmed for centuries. Long before that, locals practiced horseback racing and fighting on the meadows here. According to local historian O. Olafsen, that is the derivation of the name Rossvoll. (Archives of the Olav H. Hauge Centre, Ulvik, Norway.)

Luminous Spaces

Table of Contents

Slowly the Woods Redden in the Gorge
Seint rodnar skog i djuvet (1956)

On the Eagle's Perch / *På ørnetuva* (1961)

Ask the Wind / Spør vinden (1971)

Gleanings / Janglestrå (1980)

Introduction:
Poetry That Opens Luminous Spaces

Olav Grinde

Overleaf: Photo: Morten Krogvold

While traveling in Donegal twenty-five years ago, I stumbled upon an Irish music and literature festival and met Michael Hartnett, one of the country's leading Gaelic poets. When he heard I was from Norway, his eyes lit up. "Have you heard of Olav H. Hauge? The apple grower who writes some of the best poetry being written in Europe today?"

I was astounded; at the time my focus was on another Norwegian poet, Rolf Jacobsen. It turned out that Hauge as well had been translated into twenty or so languages.

When younger Norwegian writers, such as Jan Erik Vold and Paal-Helge Haugen, discovered Olav H. Hauge in the mid-1960s, they celebrated his "thing"– poems – embracing him as one of their own. However, I think Hauge is more accurately described as a poet of luminous spaces.

Hauge defies easy labels. Is he a Classicist or a Romantic? It can be argued that he is both. He is a Modernist who wrote sonnets all his life, and with the mocking and self-ironic "Old Poet Tries His Hand as a Modernist," he chafed at the idea of being categorized.

Although Hauge died in 1994, I speak of his poems in the present tense, because they continue to echo – transporting the reader to luminous spaces, as in "Ocean":

> Look, says the gleaming ocean,
> I too have stars
> and blue depths.

Olav H. Hauge was born on 18 August 1908 in Ulvik, the fjordside village where he spent almost his entire life. His middle initial stands for Håkonson, a patronym that reflects ancient naming traditions. While his mother Katrina had deep roots in Ulvik, his father, Håkon, four years her junior, came from Sogn, several mountain ranges and one fjord farther north.

Olav was one of the four siblings that survived childhood, the others being Pål, Anna, and Oddmund. The death of three other siblings – when Olav was eight, ten and twelve years old – made a deep impression on him. In one early poem he speaks of:

Black crosses
in white snow,
leaning over in rain.

The young schoolboy quickly became good friends with the town librarian, who helped guide him to the classics of the national, Nordic and world literatures. And Hauge became an avid reader of newspapers and literary magazines. He would sometimes sneak away from farm chores, climbing a nearby pine tree to immerse himself in worlds opened up by the printed word. His parents often indulged him.

In his diary Hauge recalls writing his first poem when he was twelve, recounting how pleasingly balanced it looked on the page with lines of roughly equal length.

Like other students, Hauge learned English and German in school, thereby expanding his horizon to additional literatures. His mother's brother, Edmund Hakestad, corresponded with the young Hauge and sent him books from America. One treasured volume at a time, Hauge collected books of literature, essays, history and philosophy– not just in Norwegian, but also in Danish, Swedish, English, German and French. The author's personal library was to become unrivalled – at least in Norway.

Due to health issues and his struggles with math, Hauge's formal education ended with junior high school. In 1929, at the encouragement of his parents, especially his mother, Hauge enrolled in the horticultural and agricultural school at Hjeltnes. In his journal he lamented: "I guess I had better put literature and language on the shelf. Soon I shall have forgotten it all." However, while studying horticulture, Hauge worked on numerous farms, including the vicarage of Ulvik, to whose library he was given access. Books were the most important ingredients in the young man's life. To say that he was impressionable would be an understatement; he proved himself to be a master autodidact, teaching himself French just by reading.

As an adult, Hauge worked as a horticulturalist and orchardist in Ulvik. When his elder brother, Pål, inherited the family farm, a smaller plot of land called Rossvoll was sectioned off and a house (*kårhus*) was built for their parents, as was the custom in Norwegian farming society. For many years Olav lived here as well, and when his father died, he inherited Rossvoll and took care of his mother. For the rest of his life, he made a meager living as an apple grower on his five acres.

The panoramic view from this farm, perched above the village, takes in the changing seasons and the many moods of the fjord and surrounding mountains. Yet even with his eyes closed the poet was intimately familiar with his surroundings:

> Lying in bed, I hear the fishermen
> head out for brisling. All night they will
> glide back and forth with their floodlights
> searching the fjord.

In April 1939, the publisher Norli rejected what could have been Hauge's first collection of poetry, tentatively titled *The Willow Flute.* They found it "unextraordinary." From what Hauge writes in his journals, he was not surprised.

The revised title of his first book, *Embers in the Ashes,* published in 1946, may be read as an image of hope. After five years' occupation by Nazi Germany, with many cities and towns bombed or torched, Norway faced the daunting task of reconstruction. In "The Fire" Hauge underscores that what is required is the flame that we carry:

> Lord, let that fire burn
> – it's a sacred guest.
> Let me glow until
> my ashes rest.

and:

> You can quench
> but never kindle
> that sacred glow.

Most of the poems in this first collection are traditional in their form, modeled on the likes of Shelley, whom he called "the bard of my youth." A notable exception is "Foxgloves in the Gravel Pit," which shows Hauge's astounding ability of observation:

The gravel pit lies there
abandoned and bare,
a spot of shame in the forest
– here a varied wilderness
begins to grow; that's how
mountain avens found hollows
below the glaciers, and that's how
alpine flowers found their place
high up on steep slopes.

. . .

Toppled tree stumps slip,
patches of sod slide down
furrows into the sandpit,
loose brush and small pines
settle in the gravel,
leaves and twigs
settle in the sand
and dissolve into loam.

Embers in the Ashes, published when he was thirty-eight years old, includes poems Hauge wrote when he was far younger. In fact, his first poem appeared in print in a newspaper in 1927 when he was only nineteen. Thus Hauge's literary production spans almost seventy years.

His second collection, *Beneath the Crag* (*Under bergfallet*) appeared in 1951. Here, a greater portion of the poems is in free verse, and we hear more clearly Hauge's unique voice, growing in strength. He says, as much to himself as to the reader:

This is your path.
Only you
shall walk it. And there is
no turning back.

And:

First thought – try
  to hold that.
The shooting star
  that lit up your mind.

However, in the telling title poem "Beneath the Crag" he also observes:

. . .there are times
you lie awake
listening
for stones falling
through the night.

In "Kin," five years later in *Slowly the Woods Redden in the Gorge,* Hauge dryly observes:

If you're kin to the pine,
you too will persist,
and the scrawnier your soil
the longer you'll last.
. . .

If you're kin to nard-grass,
you'll last the longest.
Splintery yellow, green-bearded,
full of rage and tough as hell.

Hauge made his living as an apple grower. He had roughly two hundred trees on his steep five-acre farm. Ulvik is at the heart of Norway's apple-growing region, the sheltered fjordscape of Hardanger. Here, a mild climate and long summer days – with up to twenty hours of sunlight – result in exceptionally aromatic fruit. The first apple seeds were planted by Cistercian monks in the thirteenth century; the monks of this order, who came from Lysekloster Monastery south of Bergen, established a large grange at Opedal, south of Ulvik, on the shores of a different branch of the Hardangerfjord.

There is nothing romantic about being an apple grower. In his journals, Hauge speaks repeatedly of how the chores in his orchard would get in the way of other things he preferred to do – his reading and his writing. And more than once he declined invitations to literary events because farm tasks needed doing at certain times. Nonetheless, Hauge continued as an orchardist long after his poetry gave him sufficient income for a livelihood.

Hauge writes about "Shaking the Snow Off Young Trees" in his orchard, looking ahead to their maturity:

> Trees that have borne a crop
> can hold a load of snow
> and think nothing of it.

He writes about "Green Apples," and about his regret at chopping down "The Big Apple Tree Outside My Window" that obscured the view:

> I don't want to admit it, but I miss that apple tree.
> Things are not the same here. It gave shelter against the wind and
> good shade, letting patches of sunlight slip through its branches
> onto my table. At night I often lay listening
> to the rustling leaves.

These poems speak of the apple grower's deep empathy for his trees, and it is from this point of view his journal entries often voice complaints about the weather.

On an autumn day in 1965, a half dozen young authors headed by Jan Erik Vold and Paal-Helge Haugen walked into the editor's office of *Profil*, the University of Oslo's literary magazine, announced that its quality was abhorrent, and that they were taking over. Incredibly enough, the current editor invited the rebels to join him. However, not all contemporary literature met with their disapproval – most of a whole issue was soon devoted to Olav H. Hauge. In particular, the new *Profil* writers celebrated *On the Eagle's Perch*, which Hauge had published in 1961, a book that won the Norwegian Critics' Award.

In the lead article, *Profil* lauded Hauge for his focus on ordinary everyday life and the world of objects. Jan Erik Vold, in particular, also praised Hauge's next volume, *Droplets On the Eastern Wind* (1971) for poems such as "Sledgehammer," "Saw," and "Scythe":

> Rrrip,
> says the saw.
> Fine firewood.
> She speaks
> her mind, that saw.

Likewise the poem "The Cat," which is even shaped like a cat:

> The cat is
> sitting in the
> farmyard when you come.
> Speak a little with the cat. More than anyone
> he senses what's really going on.

Many of the *Profil* authors became known for political poems or novels with strong political agendas. Only very occasionally does Hauge refer to world events. Notable exceptions are Korea and Vietnam.

Hauge touches on the immediate – whether tools and other objects, the landscape, farm tasks such as haying, or his regret at having chopped down an old apple tree. He also refers to everyday or odd occurrences, such as a bullet from the war suddenly dropping onto the floor of his hallway.

As mentioned earlier, Hauge chafed at the idea of being categorized. In his self-ironic poem "Old Poet Tries His Hand as a Modernist" he writes:

> He too was determined to try
> these new stilts.
> He's hoisted himself up,
> strides warily as a stork.
> Amazing how far-sighted he is.
> He can even count his neighbor's sheep.

According to Hauge, the lion's share of the poems in *Droplets on the Eastern Wind* (1966) came to him over a month-long period. This is incredible given not only that this book is his longest, but according to most critics also his strongest. Certainly in terms of gaining a large national audience it was his breakthrough publication. This book contains English translations of ninety of its one-hundred-and-seven poems.

Some are very short poems that echo the Imagists, as well as Japanese Haiku poets. (In the 1960s, numerous volumes of Chinese and Japanese poetry were published in Norwegian translation.) In fact, Hauge's very title hints at this fertile source. However, as Idar Stegane, one of the foremost Hauge scholars, says: "In western Norway, it rarely rains when the wind is easterly, but should raindrops be carried from that direction, the rainfall is usually all the more dear."

It might be argued that Hauge reaches for the traditional symbols of Far Eastern poetry – moon, cloud, mountain, river, tree, garden, orchard, fruit – but these are no farther away than his own back yard and the view beyond. Hauge may use these familiar images, but in a way that is novel and transformative. For instance, in speaking of his search for Truth:

> Don't give me the whole truth,
> don't give me the ocean for my thirst,
> don't give me heaven when I ask for light,
> but give me a glint, a dewdrop, a speck,
> just as the birds carry droplets of water from their bathing
> or the wind a grain of salt.

Hauge is a master at erasing the distance between his reader and the subject matter. In "Swine", from his next collection *Ask the Wind* (1971), his vivid details of horrific events and the darker aspects of history, such as the aftermath of Gettysburg, create an overwhelming immediacy:

> I come across a flock of black swine rooting
> in the stomachs of the dead and injured – they raise
> their crimson muzzles and look suspiciously
> from the edge of this circle of light
> falling from my reading lamp.

Another breakthrough, this time in his personal life, occurred several years after this publication. In 1975, artist and master weaver Bodil Cappelen moved to Ulvik. Soon Hauge built an annex onto his house with a studio for her. When they were married three years later, Hauge was seventy years old. He penned a number of poems to her, including "Looking at the Postmark of Your First Letter," "For Bodil Who Sent Me an LP of Bach and Handel," and "That One Word."

In his years with Bodil, the poet showed a greater willingness to travel from his native Hardanger. He tells of journeying northward to pass the Arctic Circle, and of Stare Miąsto in Warsaw; previously he rarely traveled far and was more inclined to write about "Coming Home."

In "One Word" he writes with a new sense of playfulness:

> This is what I wanted
> to say to her.
> That one word.
> But it has to be
> just a hint,
> a trace,
> a riddle,
> a dream
> – it must come
> like a wing

at night –
come as the wind
with eyes
of oceans and stars.

Idar Stegane, a lifelong friend of Hauge and one of Norway's foremost experts on the poet, divides Hauge's poetry and spiritual growth into three stages: "Fallen from grace," "The solitary outsider,"and "At home on this Earth." Certainly this third stage coincides with the happy years he spent with Bodil.

Many people tried to interview Olav H. Hauge; not all have been equally successful. Karl Ove Knausgård, author of the six-volume autobiographical novel *My Struggle*, recalls the time that he visited the author, bringing two friends. Hauge, who was only expecting Knausgård, stared at the overwhelmingly large delegation. Finally he said, "Well, I guess you should come inside." And inside, one of Knausgård's friends brought out his camera, asking Hauge to reposition himself to where the light was better, to which Hauge replied, "No one is taking any damned pictures here." Knausgård's other friend paged through his notes and asked a long, intricate question. Hauge stared at the floor a long time and then, without looking up, said, "I don't talk about my poems."

Knausgård has a very telling sentence in his story: "Hauge was a dweller of the spirit, steadfast and uncompromising, whereas I was merely a tourist of the spirit. And I had brought my friends to inspect this phenomenon." Surely Hauge sensed that – and responded accordingly.

When I visited the poet in 1990, with Dennis Maloney and Elaine LaMattina of White Pine Press, Hauge took us on a walk to visit a neighboring farmer, who brought a piece of carved wood out from his barn. It was from Ulvik stave church, built in the early 1200s and torn down in 1711. Such relics, which one would normally expect to find in a museum, have been treasured by locals and passed down for generations.

Not all treasures that are passed down are visible. *Nynorsk,* the language of Hardanger and much of rural Norway, has been honed through hundreds of generations. Like an old tool handle, it fits the hand and has great utility. And like an ancient pine, it is part of the very landscape, embracing the crag or rocky soil on which it stands. *Nynorsk* was not only the spoken language that Hauge grew up with, but he belonged to the first generations of children who learned and used *Nynorsk* in school. To this tongue he remained loyal, but it was definitely a handicap in gaining a wide readership. Moreover, for years Hauge's audience was limited by his uncompromising insistence on the "old orthography" of 1917 and his use of a vocabulary that many modern Norwegians found obscure and esoteric. Translators are not the only ones reaching for a dictionary!

Ironically *Nynorsk* means "new Norwegian." This written language, developed by the brilliant linguist Ivar Aasen (1813–1896), is based on rural dialects and is thus closer to Old Norse and far older than the Danish-influenced *Bokmål* (literally, the language of the book). After the Black Death decimated Norway's population, the country was weakened. From 1380 and until 1814, it was ruled by Denmark – 434 years in all. The bureaucracy as well as the clergy were Danish, or at least educated in Denmark. This created a polarization between city dwellers and the people of rural Norway which persists to this day.

So *Nynorsk,* with its direct lineage to Old Norse, is essentially a language of country people and values, while *Bokmål,* the urban dialect, may be a language of the educated but also embodies a debt to the Danish. Hauge's insistence on writing in *Nynorsk* is both a political and social statement about what it is to be Norwegian.

Ivar Aasen not only compiled a new written language, publishing his dictionary and grammar in 1850, but was also the first *Nynorsk* poet. His was an era of Norwegian national reawakening and many other writers proudly followed in Aasen's footsteps, including Kristofer Uppdal (1878–1961), turning their back on the Dano-Norwegian *Bokmål.* Hauge continued this proud tradition.

Olav H. Hauge played a major role in the translation of world poetry into Norwegian. From English, he translated Shakespeare, Alfred Tennyson,

William Butler Yeats, Robert Browning, Stephen Crane, Sylvia Plath, and Robert Bly. His German translations include Friedrich Hölderlin, Georg Trakl, Paul Celan, Johannes Bobrowski, and Bertolt Brecht. From French, he rendered poems by Paul Verlaine, Stéphane Mallarmé, Arthur Rimbaud, Francis Ponge, Henri Michaux and René Char.

Interestingly, one of the first poems by Hauge to appear in print was his translation of "Home No More Home To Me" by Robert Louis Stevenson. This is also a lesson in the difficulties and dilemmas of translation; Hauge's version of the title means simply "homeless."

He himself wrote poems in homage to other European poets: William Blake, Georg Trakl, Bertolt Brecht, Paul Celan, Gérard de Nerval and Iceland's Einar Benediktsson. Another poem celebrates Emily Dickinson, and yet another the tenth-century Norse poet Egil Skallagrímsson.

While Hauge admired the visionary Blake, the French symbolists, and other early Modernists as well as some contemporary poets, it is worth noting that his literary horizon was hardly limited to Europe. From an early date he was seeking inspiration from Chinese poetry and Japanese *haiku*. Hauge dedicates poems to great Chinese authors such as Ch'ü Yüan, Li Po, and T'ao Ch'ien. To the latter, who was legendary not only for his poetry but also for his keen appreciation of wine, Hauge writes:

> Should T'ao Ch'ien
> come to visit someday, I will
> show him my cherry and apple trees;
> I hope he'll come in the spring
> when they're in bloom. Then we'll sit in the shade
> with a glass of cider, perhaps I'll show him
> a poem – if I can find one he'd like.
> The dragons that blazed across the sky, trailing smoke and poison,
> soared more quietly in his day, and more birds sang.
> There's nothing here he wouldn't understand.

In addition, Hauge's journals reveal that Eastern spiritual traditions held a lifelong fascination for him.

Comparisons between Olav H. Hauge and the Spanish poet Antonio Machado are also in order. Both authors have left us masterful poems where the spaces between words are luminous and full of song.

Hauge's first book, *Embers in the Ashes*, appeared in 1946, and his last, *Gleanings (Janglestrå)*, was released in 1980, a span of thirty-four years. Nevertheless his poetic production spans a far longer period. The first book covers twenty years and includes poems that can be dated as far back as 1927. He constantly revised *Collected Poems (Dikt i samling)*, and edited five of the six editions published, often with the subtitle *New and Expanded*. Right up until his death, Hauge revised his poems. He deleted some and added others to his books – not just new ones at the end of his *Collected Poems* but to all of his books, reflecting when the poem in question was first written.

This book also contains translations of fourteen uncollected poems, found posthumously amongst his manuscripts and made available by his widow, Bodil Cappelen. Three of these were written in Hauge's journals and the other eleven found in his other manuscripts.

Hauge's journals, which were published posthumously, comprise over four thousand pages and span seventy years, from 1924, when he was just fifteen years old, to 1994. It is one of the largest such diaries from a major European author. While the journals give us a fascinating insight into Hauge's personal and poetic development, his daily life, his moods and emotional challenges, readers looking for cultural gossip, confessions and accusations will search in vain.

A generous selection of journal entries have been translated for this book, and are placed immediately prior to the section of poems from the same period. Hauge's journals include a number of fine poems not published elsewhere, some of which are here presented in their own right.

Our excerpts reveal the range of Hauge's thoughts and concerns. Not only do his journals complement and yield insights into Hauge's poetry, at times his entries rise to pure poetry.

In many poems we sense Hauge's heightened awareness of the moment, but he never turns his back on the ordinary. On the surface, the subject matter may seem mundane, but by pulling our awareness to the everyday and to the things that surround us, Hauge renews the world for us. The poet speaks from a luminous space and invites the reader to enter. Likewise he lends a transcendent quality to ordinary tasks: "Opening the Curtains," inspecting the scythes, "Emptying the Ash-drawer," seeing "Two Rowboats on the Fjord," or simply "Pausing Beneath an Old Oak on a Rainy Day." Other poems speak of his cat, a squirrel, that intrepid bird the dipper, crows, seagulls, owls, the spider, and the dung beetle. But also a weed growing by a rock.

Like few others, Hauge brings the landscape alive: the nearby waterfall, the rotting tree stump, a wobbly boulder, mountain pastures and hayfields. And on a northern mountain slope, the snowfield that never totally disappears.

He writes also of everyday things that might seem common but that to the observant reader yield many insights into the culture of Hauge's Hardanger. He dedicates poems to his scythe and sledgehammer, the sawbuck, his axe and chopping block – but also to the stretched wire onto which hay is hung to dry for winter fodder.

It should come as no surprise that Hauge's poetic awareness embraces the ancient – a trapping pit, a stone grave, the discovery of an old dugout boat, the changing vegetation of an abandoned mountain farm – and stories and legends that still resonate – of Orvar Odd, Leiv Eiriksson, the mythical King Sveigðir. As Idar Stegane points out, in the poem "Ogmund Rides Home," Hauge presents a whole novel about this crusader in just eleven lines!

True, Hauge does not write about the Hardanger fiddle and how it inspired the compositions of Edvard Grieg, who spent much time in the region – a point that no foreign travel writer would miss. But in many of Hauge's poems we can hear music that he learned from the Norse bards!

Much has been made of Hauge's struggles with madness, and for good reason. All in all, he spent five years in Valen psychiatric hospital. The first time, he was incarcerated for three and a half years, starting in 1934. Throughout his life, Hauge's journal entries speak of deep doubts, and of "the other man," who according to Hauge was everything he was not. Also some poems hint of this, for instance "The Shadow" from his 1946 collection:

> Poor shadow! Don't mind
> if I smile at you,
> for I myself am the shadow
> of another.

At almost precisely five-year intervals, Hauge suffered a mental crisis. Strikingly, his episodes coincide with the five-year cycle of his book publications. When Hauge was overwhelmed, for instance when he was completing a new book of poems, he would forget to eat, with dire consequences for his health; thus it seems no exaggeration to say that he wrote himself into madness. Hauge actually read the page proofs for his first book of poems while a psychiatric patient at Valen.

In his journal Hauge writes: "I remember standing before my window at Valen Hospital, looking out over the islands and sounds of Sunnhordland. Day after day I stood on that same spot, looking out. I was in a trance. The land and sea were blue and ethereal, a land beyond time and space.

"According to what I read, I probably suffered from schizophrenia. Catatonic schizophrenia is a diagnosis that seems to fit, but since I am doing my own analysis it may not be reliable."

Did he write poems at Valen? "Never. You cannot write poetry in that state." But peering back at Valen he wrote moving poems such as "The Wheat Field," about a print on the wall, and respectfully about his fellow patient "Old Vamråk." It is worth noting that Hauge had no more breakdowns after Bodil entered his life.

"The Cell", published posthumously, is one of the last Hauge wrote:

> I belonged here.
> Perhaps I always
> longed for here.
> A naked cell.
> Worn floorboards,

a heavy oak door
with a small slot.
. . .

Below the window
a radiator
encased in steel;
such a wondrous sound
when I beat it
and sang.

Strange marks on the wall
and letters scratched in stone.
Iron bars on the window,
but each day the sun came
and laid a golden slab
on the floor.
Here as well.

Even here Hauge found a luminous space!

In his most renowned and quoted poem, "It Is That Dream," he speaks of the yearning we all share:

It is the dream we carry
that something wonderful will happen,
that it must happen –
that time will open,
that our hearts may open,
that doors shall open,
and the mountain shall open
that springs will gush forth –
that our dream will open,
and that one morning we'll glide
into a cove we didn't know.

Foreword:
It Started with a Letter . . .

Bodil Cappelen

Overleaf: Pausing above the treeline, 1975. Bodil and Olav on a mountain hike in Austdalen, near Mount Osanuten in Ulvik. (Archives of the Olav H. Hauge Centre, Ulvik, Norway.)

On an autumn day in 1969 I found a book of poetry on sale in Arendal. The small collection, entitled *On the Eagle's Perch* (*På Ørnetuva*), was by Olav H. Hauge, whom I had heard of but never met.

I was thirty-nine at the time, lived in an old wooden house built by a ship pilot, with my husband and our two children. My husband and I were poor artists, living the life of the world's two last bohemians in the countryside.

I liked the poems I read. A few months later, in February of 1970, I wrote a letter to the poet expressing my gratitude for his book.

He answered. I had invited him to come visit us. Olav wrote that he would come in the summer, but he didn't. Just after responding to my letter, he received a letter from another woman, who was unmarried, and surely that was more interesting. Nonetheless, we continued our correspondence, with gaps of a few weeks or months. Olav was a bachelor in his sixties, living in Ulvik, the innermost village of a fjord arm of the famous Hardangerfjord. I was twenty-two years younger, a textile artist living in a nineteenth-century house by the sea. I had never imagined living anywhere else. And neither Olav nor my husband and I owned a car.

After almost five years' correspondence we finally met. Olav was going to read some of his poems at Henrik Ibsen's family farm. I waited for the poet as agreed, beneath a large ash tree, and then he walked into my life!

Soon our letters became much more frequent. In January of 1975 I received a poem in the mail.

Carpet

Weave me a carpet, Bodil,
weave it of dreams and visions,
weave it of wind,
so that I, like a Bedouin, may
unroll it for prayer,
wrap it around myself
when I sleep,
and every morning call:
"The table is set!"
Weave it

as a cloak
against the cold,
a sail
for my boat!
One day I shall sit on that carpet
and sail away into
another world.

And then, late on an April evening that year, a van rolled into the courtyard at Rossvoll, his farm overlooking Ulvik. I sat beside a friend who had driven me and all my belongings, including my large loom, all the way from Kalvøysund on that island near Arendal.

Thus started our nineteen years together. I wove and painted; Olav carried on with his tasks, read and wrote. Together we tended his orchard, picked raspberries and black currants, and planted potatoes. I tended the flowers in the garden. "They haven't been cared for since the war," he said with satisfaction.

In May of 1994, Olav died peacefully in his own bed at Rossvoll. All together he had spent six years in a psychiatric hospital, in his youth and as an adult. That was more than enough. He wanted to die at home.

One day, while sitting there alone in that house, I thought of all the letters we wrote to each other through the years. I had brought mine to Rossvoll. Had he kept his, I wondered. He had indeed. They were bundled in a box in the attic. I sorted them chronologically, and read each letter in turn, mine and his. That was quite an experience! This is like a novel in letter form, I thought.

Thinking others might find that "novel" rewarding, I sent those letters to Olav's publisher. In 1998 it was published: *Olav H. Hauge – Bodil Cappelen, Letters 1970 – 75*.

There is a riddle in our story. How could this man, who so needed and cherished his solitude, take the drastic step of inviting a woman to live with him, for the rest of their days? Was it as simple as he wrote in his letter? "If you want to move here, that's fine."

Nobody understood that.

Many years later I found a small yellow notebook amongst Olav's papers. Most of the cover had been cut off; I suppose he used the cardboard for something else, perhaps to write a poem. On the first page was written *Dreams.* The first was a dream from the 20th of March, 1964, followed by twenty dreams from that same year. There is a gap and then more dreams from 1974 and 1975.

The last he wrote was:

> "Dreamt of Bodil. When I woke it was as though her arms still embraced me, although she was gone." (16 February 1975)
>
> "Dreamt of Bodil. She was here again. And still here when I awoke! Three nights in a row this happened. Vividly powerful dreams!" (17 February)

I opened the book of our letters and there it was: "Bodil! There was something I meant to say (Perhaps you understood that?) before you left: If you want to move here, that's fine."

That first time, as I was about to walk through the door into Olav's home, when I visited that autumn of 1974, I felt nervous and full of awe. It was as though a flock of birds were repeatedly calling out in my head: "Here you shall live, here you shall live, here you shall live!" "Surely not! Stop that!" I called back. Then I stepped through that door.

On a day in the autumn, that year Olav died, I felt it was time. I pulled open a heavy drawer of the desk where Olav kept his journals. He had kept a diary since 1924, when he was sixteen years old. The last entry was written ten days before he died. Those eighty-three notebooks covered seventy years.

No one came to disturb me. I read without interruption. Olav had told me he had long pondered what to do with his journals when I came to share his bed and board and to wander through the house.

He had never shown them to anyone. Should he keep them hidden, write his entries secretly from now on? No, he couldn't be bothered. "If she wants to read them, then so be it."

Sometimes his journal lay on the table in our living room, sometimes on his night table. "There is an ink spot on the duvet cover," I said. "Well, we'll just have to live with that. This Parker pen is great for writing."

Olav's journals were published by Samlaget in the year 2000. Five volumes, each about a thousand pages.

And the story continues.

It continues in the form of poems and journal entries, translated for new readers.

–Bodil Cappelen
Son, Norway

Embers In the Ashes

Glør i oska

1946

Overleaf: The young Hauge in a rowboat, 1932, during his horticultural studies. Taken at Njøs Farm, Hermansverk in Sogn, the district where his father grew up. (Archives of the Olav H. Hauge Centre, Ulvik, Norway.)

Excerpts from Hauge's Journals
– through autumn 1946

March 1924

Words to a Diary – A thought struck me the other day: I shall keep a journal. It should be fun. Yes, not a journal in the usual sense of the word, with weather forecasts, events, purchases and tasks. No, this shall be a journal of thoughts and reflections – a spiritual journal – of what might be worth remembering. It does not need to be every day, with numbered days and the like. Rather I shall write when I have time, and during the weekends and such. There should be joy in this. I need paper; the best thing would be to buy a large book with lined pages. I'll see what I can find. Perhaps I can also, in this same book, write down my thoughts about various books. I'll think about it!

May 1924

Walked in the mountains today, first time this spring.

Thoughts like potent dreams rose within me. I wish I could build here and live here, a place to be alone with my thoughts!

To be able to sit there, looking out over the wind rustling through the leaves of wooded hills, letting my eyes glide over old swaying pine forests. They have atmosphere, and a there is a restful, eternal peace beneath huge, swaying trees.

And then, behind it all and furthest removed from human eyes – the mountains – restful, sky-blue, pure; appearing from a dreamy mist and blue-grey heavens. You reach up towards eternity! Showing us the path, the path to eternity – that is where I long to be!

I want to pull myself up there, away from the narrow-mindedness down here, where no one understands me! There I would ride forth under a bright sun, toward mountains and heavens that fade into blue, riding a snow-white, downy-light and floating cloud, gazing out over everything. Yes, there must be flight, and air under my wings for feelings, and thoughts – higher than everything.

Up there my mind should be able to compose a song!

March 1925

I am writing an English letter to America, and it is going well. I see now that it is possible to learn a foreign language on your own – if you set your mind to it. When I have learned English fairly well, I would like to learn another. Perhaps Spanish or French, and German should not be ignored. And then I would like to learn Latin, Hebrew, and Classical Greek. I've heard that makes people clever!

I must get ahold of the instruction books! Yes, on my own I'm reading up to be a professor, and it's going well! As though it matters! "This boy has got what it takes!"

August 1927

I am nineteen now. You age before you know it. Mercilessly slowly the days pass, the months and years – even though Einstein says time does not exist!

November

It is already late autumn
and things are as they usually are at this time.
The wind from the mountain plateau, empty and cold,
squelches each spark of life
and mist creeps down the hills.

It is late autumn now,
and every sun-ray of summer is gone.
Rainshowers fall on desolate hills,
mountains turn white with new snow,
and mist glides down over the farm.

–O. Hauge 1927

I am not out every day; I prefer sitting at home. They call me a lone wolf, I suppose. I don't feel at ease anywhere! Oh, people! I do not know you! You are not like I thought. I freeze amongst you and feel lonelier than when I am alone …

From where did I know you? From that strange, secret dream world of childhood. But the world is otherwise. I cannot recognize anything, not even myself. Oh, the dream world of my childhood! Perhaps you were the only right one? Is it the treasures gathered then that should provide sustenance that we should later live on?

March 1929
"The wanderer must knock on many doors, and wander past many houses, in order to find his own home."
(Rabindranath Tagore, *Gitanjali*)

I have started my studies at Hjeltnes Horticultural School. I guess I had better put literature and language on the shelf. Soon I shall have forgotten it all.

April
Home again! The other day I put the axe into my leg just above the knee, and naturally I had to go to bed.

1929
Melancholy must be an illness. There are many melancholy moments – moments where everything you love becomes "utter Nothingness," as Walt Whitman writes. My spiritual life is an endless fluctuation between light and shadow... Sometimes I feel lonely in the night, separated from everything that binds me to life; all reality floats before me as though it were a strange dream. Is this how it should be? It is strange how all moods have their own beauty and their own delight.

I have heard much talk of "spirit" and "soul," but I have never been able to understand what those words really mean. When I think or speak I sense that this isn't really me. There must be something greater, something more, than this outer "shell" that functions in the grey, everyday life. What is it? Is it "soul" or "spirit"? If I contemplate this as best I can, I manage only to tie myself into a knot of feelings, unclear impressions, hopes and desires, both good and bad. With influence from outside, a simple mood can burn so intensely that it alone seizes power. This I know, as well as many other psychological facts; but still: What is the soul? Is it a finer organism clothed in a material body? A reflection of the external world? Certainly it is all this, but isn't it something more? Perhaps our soul cannot be comprehended, cannot be held nor embraced by our material means?

Let poetry be a starry vault over the soul!

> I believe in you my soul...
> Loaf with me on the grass, loose the stop from your throat,
> to song ...
>
> –Walt Whitman

11 March 1934

Have just passed the Examination at the Horticultural School at Hjeltnes. The result was fairly good. I got ill and had a bad time during the examination days. Have recovered a little.

20 October 1937

It is, indeed, a long time since I wrote a word in my diary. Several years, I think. Many things have happened, many good days have passed since I wrote last time. Let me recall those memorable days at Hjeltnes. In due time after the Examination I returned to Hermansverk. I had got a severe cold and went suddenly mad. Completely. My father was asked to come, and he was compelled to bring me to an asylum in Bergen. Having been there a short time, I recovered a little, but I had a new attack and was then brought to Valen Hospital. There I have stayed all the time except for a few months spent at home. I am sorry to say that my father found he could not have me at home. On 19 August 1937, however, I was returned and am now in fairly good health, I think.

30 January 1938

To grow angry and let the daily trivialities run off with one's temper, is a most annoying thing. The unfeeling that immediately follows an outburst of stinginess is distastrous in the long run. I read recently in the papers that this is a frequent germ of insanity. Usually one feels physically sick afterwards. Be on guard.

7 May

I put together a collection of my poems, calling it *The Willow Flute.* I suppose there are around sixty poems.

17 April 1939

Norli publishers returned my collection, *The Willow Flute.* They said my poems were good, but hardly extraordinary. Didn't expect any better either.

10 June 1944

The village is all in bloom. Everything is blossoming this year: the fruit trees, rowan, and bird cherry. In the last few days, ash and oak have sprouted leaves. They are late, especially the ash. It doesn't put its leaves out until it can trust the weather.

Window - I haven't had anything else to occupy me for a long time now. From my sickbed I can see the landscape through the window. A Norwegian landscape. First the wooded slope with pines and scattered birch – then the sparse mountain forest above that, and at last the barren mountain, hard and black, with a strip of changing sky above it all.

Through these three windowpanes I can see no more than that. But it is enough. I have lain here a long time and looked out every day. Today it was rainy and grey; this evening it's sunny. I lie here, building my castles over there. Autumn has arrived. Yellow birches stand luminous on still days, and rowan trees add color, lighting things up here and there.

26 June

There is not much to write about during the grey existence of a worker, least of all poetry. Cracked hands, aching back, illness and complaints, these I see and know. But poetry? No.

June

The Loafer – I won't mention any names. I'll call him the Loafer. True enough, people fault him and call him an idler. He doesn't watch his money, works little, and drinks. That may be so. But the man may still have his good sides. I think he is knowledgeable, humoristic and wise, with tolerance and wisdom like few others. That's because he has more time to read and think than others do. This, however, is the way it is: in order to be seen as a good man, you must be diligent, thrifty, temperate, morally flawless and preferably god-fearing as well. The good villagers have no other measure of a man. Knowledge and wisdom count for little.

5 July

Haymaking – Almost done bringing in the dried hay now, but some of the racks are in such steep terrain that there is no getting to them by horse and cart. Burning hot sun. Hunch-backed and with splayed legs, I stagger up the path in those outfields. The rope digs through my thin shirt into sore red flesh, the straws prick and poke. My burden sags lower and lower toward the ground, and my neck is stretched like on a nosy gossip. Before long it feels like I'm carrying all the burdens of this world. Panting with my tongue out, I stagger up the ramp and collapse in the barn.

6 July

To a Good Friend —You have the whole world before you. It is yours, God's green earth. I have only a sheet of white paper. That's where I shall live. That is where I shall love, hate, write. That's where I shall build my castles and realize my dreams.

July

Moral Epistles to Lucilius by Seneca is very interesting. So young and fresh and modern! And such a stylist! Seneca is the father of many aphorisms. His style is pointed and paradoxical, lively and colorful. A good example of how form matters as much as content.

De Rerum Natura (*On the Nature of Things*) – None of the classical poets seem as modern as Lucretius, none stands closer to us. Goethe had a keen appreciation of him. I have just read a new translation of one of Lucretius' main works. It could well have been written today.

30 October

I hope the war ends soon, so I can buy books from abroad. I miss writers such as Shelley and Burns, and many of the French: La Bruyère, France, Hugo, Verlaine.

1 November
How can it be that sometimes we are so lucid and eager to work, while other times we feel that our imagination and thoughts are blocked? Could the reason be physiological?

Perhaps. Or it may be that this is the rhythm of life itself, shifting like high and low tide?

Reading – I can't stomach having to read long, stupid novels just to find a few lines of poetry and true feeling. I would rather go to the masters of verse, those who have kept the poetry and cut away the rest.

The difference between the wise man and others is that he follows his own thoughts, while the others have their eyes on their neighbor.

8 April 1945
Peace at last. People are gathering around those who have a radio, listening. Churchill spoke at three o'clock today. Just as dogged as last time I heard him. The surrender has been signed in Rheims, and today it will be ratified in Berlin.

9 April
It sounds like we have won our freedom back. There are gunshots and tiny explosions throughout the village. It seems a strange way to celebrate the peace, but many people like fingering and playing with weapons. I would have thought they'd had enough of gunshots and explosions. But I suppose there is satisfaction in doing what you like.

Black Crosses

Black crosses
in white snow,
leaning over in rain.

The dead came here
across bramble-filled moors
carrying crosses on their shoulders,
they set them down
and went to rest,
each beneath
their icy mound.

Toward Snowy Peaks

Toward snowy peaks
and chasm's night,
I followed
my vision's way.
Once more
I take to the road
– for I am a stranger
to this world.

The fire that burned
has died down,
quenched the star
that guided me.
And here is no one,
no peace.
But dire need gave
many a man
his grit.

The Fire

Sacred was the fire
that burned in your heart.
Fool, you failed to fathom,
tried to quench the flame.
You carried water to that fire,
water and sand.

Humbly you should have prayed,
your hands a nest:
Lord, let that fire burn
– it's a sacred guest.
Let me glow until
my ashes rest.

Fool you were who
failed to fathom the brink.
So now you eat and drink
and sleep in peace.
You can quench
but never kindle
that sacred glow.

The Shadow

Poor shadow, you have
the shape of a man, but no life!
It is touching to see
how much you try to
resemble me, try to do
as I do:
you rest your head on your hand,
sit and brood,
you grip your pen and write –
rise from the table,
go out and walk
halt in deep thought, stand there
still as a stone.
A call sounds in the heart;
did you see the wings of thought
shining sharply?

Poor shadow! Don't mind
if I smile at you,
for I myself am the shadow
of another.

Foxgloves in the Gravel Pit

A gaping gash in
the forest, a torn wound,
chaotic and collapsed,
tufts of grass hang from
caved-in edges;
a steam shovel and
huge piles of stone
burn hot red in the sun;
flakes of mica
flash and glitter in
the rain-washed ground,
a wheelbarrow
sticks up out of the sand,
rotting bits of plank
lie strewn about.

Surrounded by outfields
and rough terrain.
By the paths and fields
are blackberry thickets
and young birches with
grass licking their legs.
The gravel pit lies there
abandoned and bare,
a spot of shame in the forest
– here a varied wilderness
begins to grow; that's how
mountain avens found hollows
below the glaciers, and that's how
alpine flowers found their place
high up on steep slopes.

Help to sow afresh: lives
and powerful forces are in play,
autumn wind and slashing rain.
Toppled tree stumps slip,
patches of sod slide down
furrows into the sandpit,
loose brush and small pines
settle in the gravel,
leaves and twigs
settle in the sand
and dissolve into loam,
scattered blades of grass
eke out a life amidst the stones,
here and there blue
harebells nod.

From all directions they come
and the gravel pit receives them:
wildflowers and grasses,
birds bring seeds that
take root in the sand,
blackberries come creeping
and grow into thickets.

From secret forest depths
come the foxgloves:
red grenadiers
with green spears
that storm toward their death
in the white gravel pit
– nowhere else in the forest
is there a fire such as this!

The Squirrel

Lightly he jumps
into the oak by the steps
and sets to work
in its crown
– autumn is a busy time
for a squirrel;
acorns and nuts
must be gathered
before leaves drop.

He finds a nut
to gnaw,
fluffs his tail and
sits there content.
The squirrel collects his share
of pinecones and nuts
– and he knows
a good, safe nest on
the elm-covered hillside.

From the stone stoop below
the cat stretches claws
but the squirrel pays
no heed, just gnaws and
crushes nuts:
Mouse-hunter,
you cannot reach me!
He mocks the cat with a shower
of nutshells on his nose.

When the nuts
are gone, I see him
scurry down
a long, thin branch
– then a daring jump!
With bushy tail he
steers his body
nimbly to reach
the roof edge.

From there he scurries
to fence and pollard birch,
barely touching ground,
then darts in a circle through
brushwood and heather.
Last I saw him
he waved his bushy tail
and jumped into
the hazel thicket.

Always I Expect to Find

Always I expect to find
something that makes life worthwhile,
something worth winning,
which shall lift me up, strengthen
my will and brace my back.

Free me from this curse of doubt
so humbly I may bend my knee
to life's eternal truth, let it
guide me right, give me goals
to reach for, faith and peace.

Blessed is the man who, drawn onward,
sees what is writ in the Lord's hand.
Serpent becomes staff, the burning
bush is green again. Find your path
before your severed day is here!

Prayer

New snow spreads its cloak
over the dark mountain.
This night sky opens doors to show
layer upon layer of blue.
Winter-stripped birches now wake
and new seedlings break soil.
A ripening autumn will sway
fields heavy with harvest.

Open my eyes, Oh Lord,
that I better may gaze
upon this marvel, not only
its outward glaze.
Till the last eve, fill my heart
with your song and embrace
– let breath and altar candle
together expire.

Beneath the Crag
Under bergfallet
1951

Overleaf: Checking the weather station on a spring day in 1949. Like many farmers of Western Norway, Hauge was an avid amateur meteorologist. (Archives of the Olav H. Hauge Centre, Ulvik, Norway.)

Excerpts from Hauge's Journals – through autumn 1951

One Year at Valen

20 December 1946

Embers in the Ashes – Yes, today I received the book of my poems published by Noregs Boklag. The book looks fine. Unfortunately I became ill last year and was unable to polish my manuscript as I had planned, and as advised by the publisher's consultants. I finally got better in the autumn and proofread my book at Valen.

Poetry 1946 – Never has this much poetry been published. Much of it is junk. But above them all towers Rolf Jacobsen, whose debut was *Earth and Iron* in 1933. That book of poems will endure.

That Day – Perhaps the day is not far when the excess of human beings must prepare to leave Mother Earth, just as bees leave the mother hive. It is not easy to say where the new hive may be built, but certainly there must be liveable conditions elsewhere as well. We just *need wings.* (*Modern Sciences,* "The Wings")

April 1947

Verse Form – With regards to verse, my thoughts are this: If you can manage to say what you want, there is nothing wrong with writing a sonnet or an *ottava rima* – that is, if you don't overburden your subject.

Form Once Again --Should they offer you wine, accept some and taste it. The shape of the glass, whether rounded or six-sided, is less important. But a beautiful glass increases the pleasure.

The First Commandment in Art – Be true to your experience. That is the first commandment. Don't write anything that you haven't experienced yourself. For poetry can liberate itself from experience, and live as though in a vacuum.

My Character – An old woman said: "Whenever I sit down and speak badly of people, it is not their character that emerges, but my own."

Schopenauer – Whoever does not know Schopenhauer cannot know wisdom and deep thinking; he is not yet awakened to the reality of life.

Back –-As children of earth and nature, we must look to the past to find authors who are simple enough. Contemporary writers are so intellectual and learned that we do not understand them.

1948

I have read Aslaug Blytt's book about the painter Lars Hertervig. She writes of his understanding of nature and to what degree his mental illness influenced his art. Schizophrenics often see nature differently than normal people. I remember standing before my window at Valen Hospital, looking out over the islands and sounds of Sunnhordland. Day after day I stood on that same spot, looking out. I was in a trance. The land and sea were blue and ethereal, a land beyond time and space.

I thought of this vision as I read about Lars Hertervig's art. It was during my illness that I often had moments when visions of nature completely entranced me; I had never seen a world like that. I walked from window to window and just looked and looked for days, weeks and months.

Verse, Once Again – To shape a poem is like releasing water into the mouth of a river – it will take the path that is most natural.

Plato – This spring I have read some of Plato's dialogues. Beautiful! Whoever hasn't read Plato, has yet to be born!

Emily Dickenson – If you write for others, your writings all too easily become ordinary. Emily Dickinson wrote for herself and won. The joy of creativity was enough for her; she did not need the vain pleasure of showing her work to others. Had she written for her contemporaries, her work would not have been as it is. Magnificent Emily! Greatest of poets!

Poetry – You don't write poetry; poetry writes itself in you.

1951

Thoughts – You cannot read your way to becoming a Christian or a Buddhist or the like. Life makes you so; your fate and your character make you so. Should you then later come into contact with such teachings or such a philosophy which you have arrived at on your own, then the encounter is so much more pleasant and sincere.

I have just read Christmas Humphreys' book, *Buddhism,* and this meeting with Buddhism is one of my great spiritual discoveries. For I realize that I am a Buddhist – I just haven't known it. Buddhism is a way of wisdom for human beings. May I now learn to walk the eight-fold path.

Television – What do people need television for? When you have imagination, you are equipped to fill many hours of solitude, many sleepless nights.

Gossip – Gossip is like the wind. It is sometimes impossible to know from which direction it blows, and words about a man are also like the wind – once they're out, they cannot be taken back. Controlling your tongue is a great art, and it is not quickly learned.

Many Ways to Assert Oneself – There are many ways to assert oneself, and people are like that. Children especially. *I got an apple,* a little girl may say. *Yes, but I get to ride in a car, says another.* Authors are much like children; they assert themselves as best they can. One has been to America, another to China; one has worked in the mines, another has been a sailor, a soldier; one has mastered Latin and Greek, another French and Spanish; one has studied the latest fashion of psychology, another attended Oxford; and yet another has been a pioneer.

Oh fools! Those who grab him and send him to the madhouse, and the doctors who inject him, guards who put him in restraints, what do you understand? You do not know that this particular man is having his epiphany, the biggest revelation of his life. He may hear the spirits speak, see the heavens open, encounter God. What if he forgets this world and is strange, for it takes a toll on a man to experience such things. Maybe he sees the past, perhaps the future is revealed to him; maybe he speaks with the dead, maybe nature and eternity appear to him in a new and unique way; maybe only now does he see the sacrality of life and death's mystery. And this man you would seize, submit to electroshock, put in restraints and commit to an asylum? Oh fools, do you know what you are doing? To shut him away is one thing, but anything more is a crime.

Empty Your Pockets – Share it all, says the critic. No, not everything. Every human being has his secret, his mystery, and he is meant to take this mystery to his grave. An author, too, is a human being and he shouldn't share everything. You can offer much on the altar of art, but not everything. There is a door you are not meant to open.

Thoughts – I sometimes wonder: Is the heart always right? Santayana writes that "it is wisdom to believe the heart" – and I think so, too. But is the heart always right? Is that so certain? Is it so sensitive that it can always tell you what to do? Yes, I think so, unless it is filled with evil, for that may also be the case. Annoyance, resentment and wrath may have taken root.

Sorcery – You need to practice sorcery if you are going to be a poet – in other words, to use words and phrases for their sound and mystery, without them necessarily having a rational meaning. Black magic, you say; perhaps so, but this is a great art. You need to master sorcery.

Poetry is a noble thing of which there is not enough in this world. Subtle and fine. Do not fault the man who hones his words and enables them to receive and hold noble content. Endless patience is needed. Stefan Mallarmé and Paul Valéry showed the way.

A poet should not be focused on his readers, but rather have his eyes fixed on a goal we may not know. He should be on the way, although I can just as easily think of him as coming. What I mean by that is that he should not be looking for the effect of his words, but instead concentrate on his chosen task, like a child immersed in play.

2 November 1951

Beneath the Crag – Received the book from my publisher today. A small book. With meager content.

Poetry Can Be Play – To make something beautiful, be it a small chest or a carved bird, is a beautiful thing. To write a beautiful poem is also a beautiful thing, and it need not be personal. You can write from outside yourself, as long as you convey the human. And whether you are blind or have a limp is of no relevance to your art. To conquer the personal, to keep your private grief to yourself, is necessary for a work of art that intends to delight the reader.

A Chinese Story About a Woodcarver and His Work – There is a three-thousand-year-old Chinese story about a woodcarver and his work:

This woodcarver made a great carving and all who saw it were astounded. His master, Prince Si, also saw it and asked the master carver: "What is your secret?" The woodcarver replied: "I am only a craftsman: I have no secret. There is only this: When I began to think about the work you commanded, I was too proud, and so for two days I worked to conquer this. When I thought I might be cleansed, I found that I was envious of another carver that I wanted to outdo. For two days I worked to rid myself of envy. Then I found myself yearning for praise, and strived for two days to conquer such thoughts. Then I thought about my coming gain and success, and for four days I worked hard to empty my mind. At last all that might distract me from the work had vanished. Then I went into the forest, the right tree appeared before my eyes, and there was no doubt. So I cut down the tree, set to work and carved what you see and ascribe to the spirits."

Insanity is the Highest Form of Subjectivity – Insanity is the highest form of subjectivity. To write poetry is like climbing the highest mountain: the ascent may be very strenuous, but all the more lightly you will dance downhill on your skis.

The Goose That Lay Golden Eggs – The goose with the golden egg. Old Aesop told his wife about a goose that laid one golden egg every day. The wife, however, thought that if she killed and butchered the goose, then she would get all the eggs at once. And so she did that – but inside, this goose was just like all others. This is how it is with many poets. Not being satisfied with writing a poem every now and again, they feel compelled to open up and try to reach everything at once. In other words, they butcher themselves to see what is inside.

Good Poems – A good poem is luminous on the page. Long after you have closed the book and returned it to its shelf, it shines in the lonely darkness.

The Modern Poet doesn't write in words, but rather in metaphors, with dreams, with the wind …

Old and New Times – The ancient ones filled the universe with spirits. Is this not more poetic than all our talk of natural forces?

Dew on a Spider's Web – Look how the rain has left droplets on a spiderweb spun between blades of grass. An incredible work of filigree. The droplets are in fine rows, like black pearls inlaid in silver, shining like dark eyes. This is where women found the patterns they used for bodice decorations long ago.

You don't need to live on spirit when it's not necessary, although you shall always serve it.

Your Path

No one has marked the path
you must walk
into the unknown,
into the distance.

This is your path.
Only you
shall walk it. And there is
no turning back.

Nor shall you mark
the path.
The wind will erase your tracks
through the mountain wilderness.

First Thought

First thought – try
  to hold that.
The shooting star
  that lit up your mind.

First thought – strike
  like the stooping falcon!
Don't chase like a hawk
  from tree to tree.

You cast the noose,
  think you've caught it,
try to catch it in
  snare and net.

Draw the bow, release
  your arrow from the string
– that game has
  fleet foot and wing.

First thought – long
  do its tracks glow,
yet you sit empty-handed
  with a web of words.

First thought
  draws forth others,
hounds hunting
  in the shadows.

Endure the night, keep
    the fire burning,
you may catch prey,
    but not the one.

And should the king himself
    enter – let go,
stand in the radiance
    of his first sign.

The Hands That Weave

Unknown hands
weave the tapestry
of human lives:
innocence of
child-hearts,
radiant dreams
of young minds.

And those hands
weave the deeds of life
like a Bayeux Tapestry,
but also Ophelia's
and Hamlet's fate.

The weaver's warp
is our heritage,
long threads
for future heirs.
The shuttle
carries the weft
to and fro,
lightning-quick,
our life of joy,
of grief and shame;
fate, like the beater of
a loom, beats us into
what we are.

Tear, You Needn't Fall

It was little to you
but meant much to me:
a smile when it mattered
and a handshake was all.

Tear,
you needn't fall,
I know you're salty.

The River Girl

In the bright spring eve
when the sap is rising and
birch leaves sprout,
she looses her hair
and dances and sings
before the mountain.
She has ceased to sport,
and her pale arms embrace
that iron-grey cliff
in a long, deep
icy kiss.

The Birch

Birch
in pine forest
– a green banner
when spring is young.
But the pine is
dark and glum.

The birch
persists
– at last
a bright blaze!
But the pine
is just as somber.

Then the birch sheds
its yellow leaves
and is left to stand
cold
with frost
on naked twigs.

Granite

That granite stone
cools the foundation
and binds the soil,
a lukewarm hole;
none are colder
in their winter coat,
none are warmer
when spring glows!

Bare-chested
he meets the spring sun,
and one day in March
smashes the icy shield;
deep in the cool earth
your stone-heart warms,
wakens flowers
and green grass.

Shaking the Snow Off Young Trees

What should you do when
it keeps coming down on you
– throw defiant barbs back
against the dancing
tumbling flocks,
or hunch your shoulders
and take what comes?

In the twilight I stumble forward
through the snowy orchard
with a pole,
to help.
So little
is needed:
a sharp tap
with that pole,
or a jerk
on the treetop
– and you're covered
in snow, but
the apple tree
springs erect
again.

Those young trees are so proud,
they haven't learned
to bend
to anything but the wind
– and mostly
just for fun,
for a thrill.
Trees that have borne a crop
can hold a load of snow
and think nothing of it.

Hedgehog

The other night, on my way home
I took the path across
the field where I knew
there was a spring.
That spring bubbled, gleaming
in darkness, catching the night.
Sitting by that dark mirror I saw,
quenching his thirst,

this bundle! Every spike
relaxed, at peace,
while his black snout gently
sipped his drink.
Quench your thirst! I can wait,
so patiently I stood.
Perhaps the two of us are
alike in many things.

Like me you take a liking
to strolling through the darkness
amongst autumn leaves, finding springs,
berries and such
– prefer solitary exploration. But if
someone comes too near,
we withdraw and show them
our spines.

Thin Ice

The fjord is calm
after the autumn storm.
Now it mirrors
the heavens and stars,
and the moon lends
its golden touch.

And one night
the shiny-black abyss
cloaks itself in steel
– a shield.
Now it carries birds
and stones cast
and lets fallen snow gather.
Which is land,
which is sea?

Until winter storm
and deep currents suddenly
splinter that steel surface,
grind it to shreds.

— — —

Mind, where is your peace,
your will, your bonds?
Thin ice
on this sleeping sea.

Beneath the Crag

You live beneath the crag
and you're mindful of it.
Yet you sow your field and
tread safely through your yard,
let your children play
and lie down at night as though
it were not there.

At times,
as you lean on your scythe
in the summer evening,
you'll glance up
at the crag
where they say
the crack is.
And there are times
you lie awake
listening
for stones falling
through the night.

The rockslide will come as no surprise.
But you'll carry on
clearing your green patch
beneath the crag
– as life allows.

The Volcano

Scorn me not, you
prim and proper mountains!
Through miserable me
shall burst forth
all the repressed
power of our ancient
craggy lineage.

It was not my lava,
my ash, my fire
– no more than it was yours,
but the fault was mine.

I'm merely a mountain
like other mountains,
not a riddle
and no godhead,
just a frail
burned-out heap.
But none know
better than I
what forces lie dormant
in a mountain.

Spider

Have you seen the spider
swing by its thread
above the black river gorge
– swinging in the wind
by its thin and
fragile thread,
spinning and
lowering itself
down, down.

Thus you swing
by the thread of
your thoughts
above the abyss,
safe as that spider
above the river gorge,
you trust that thread
and do not see
the gaping death
beneath.

Should that thread
be broken once,
you'll never feel
quite safe again;
that anxious scream
from when you fell
is part of you.
The breached mind
is slow to heal.

This Is Your Burden

This is your burden:
that you didn't measure up,
that you were a wavering feather
rather than a firm arrow
in the strong wind.

You didn't climb the mountain,
didn't row across the water,
didn't kill the dragon
– you didn't come when
your true love called.

Whether you faced windswept
snow, clinging fog
or pelting rain,
you should have come.
Valund suffered
severed heel tendons,
but he made himself wings.
You sat there whittling
toys for children.

In your dreams you go out,
time and again,
climbing mountains,
rowing the waters,
killing the dragon
coming to her.
Thus you try to
make your life
complete.

The Back-Cracking Hug

A back-cracking hug,
in same outfits
we grapple and bend,
the other and I,
I try to head-butt
and try to hit him,
he glides like the shadow
I cannot reach.

He's there in the flesh,
in this fool's life,
and he carves runes
with his secret knife
these facial lines
that mark each year,
he knocks out teeth
and pulls out hair.

He steals the hours,
the silent and counted,
and all my joys
he leaves them cold;
exhausted we sleep
after hard day's fight,
we must grapple again
when we wake.

He hooks his claw
in naked flesh,
the bruises ache and
the pain is sweet;
heavy-headed
of swelled anguish,
we fill the world
with towering pain.

Thus we wrestle,
thus we grapple,
a back-cracking hug;
neither will forfeit
nor release the grip,
and neither can force
the other to kneel,
till we both tumble
into the grave.

Behind the Mountain of Solitude

Solitude is sweet,
so long as the road back
to the others
is open.
You cannot shine
entirely alone.

But the day that crag
collapses
behind you,
will be the day
you stand shouting, beating
your fists against a closed wall.

And you'll lament to the stars,
stones, sea and wind,
thinking they know,
making yourself
less than them.

Oh, you behind the mountain of solitude!
Once again
a hidden river runs,
should you, like Sinbad,
dare to follow its course.

You're Still Young

You are still young and won't
understand when I speak of darkness and pain;
your day is so clear, your will yet unbroken.

We can't avoid speaking
of our grief, because it is she
who makes us what we are.

If you pass into darkness someday,
then you too must have faith in your dream,
that it will guide you, like a child guiding the blind man.

Stone God

You carry the stone god
within you.
And you serve him faithfully
and make him secret offerings.
With bloody hands
you bring him
wreaths and lit candles,
yet still you feel
his coldness
in your heart,
and you know your features
will harden like his
and your smile
be just as cold.

You Want Only to Be

Not the root groping
in hard rock,
neither sprout nor sapling,
nor the trunk in the storm,
nor the humble branch,
nor bast, nor bark
in snow and frost
– nor the rising sap,
nor the force that grows,
neither fruit nor seed,
nor the leaf silently
building its dome
– you want only to be
the beaming bloom.

Ocean

This is the ocean.
All serious,
vast and grey.
Yet just as the mind
in solitary moments
suddenly opens its
shifting reflections
to secret depths
– so the ocean, too,
one blue morning
may open itself
to sky and solitude.
Look, says the gleaming ocean,
I too have stars
and blue depths.

The Fisherman and the Sea

The sea is
mysterious in man's mind.
To be a humble fisherman
was my prayer,
my dream.

You brought
searchlights and sinkers,
wanting to drag
my sea

– drag, where
there is no bottom.
Cradle and sway, sea of my sorrow!
May the depths
and distant stars
baffle his toil.

Conch

You build the house of your soul,
and wander proudly
in the starlight
with that house on your back,
just as a snail does.
Should you sense danger,
you'll crawl inside your house
and be safe
behind its hard
shell.

And when you are no more,
that house
shall remain
and bear witness
to the beauty of your soul.
And the sea of your solitude
shall sing from
within.

Tongue and Bell

I am the tongue
within the bell,
the heavy
silent
tongue.

Don't touch me
– lest I
brush against
bronze and
splinter the
silence.

Only when the bell
starts swinging
should I beat,
swing
and beat,
on that
deep
bronze.

Slowly the Woods Redden in the Gorge

Seint rodnar skog i djuvet

1956

Overleaf: Hauge leaning on his scythe, 1956. Photo: Ola E. Bø, *Bergen Arbeiderblad.* (Archives of the Olav H. Hauge Centre, Ulvik, Norway.)

Excerpts from Hauge's Journals – through autumn 1956

1952

Strawberries – Strawberries. The first baskets picked, nothing is like these; so fresh, such virgin excitement! The berries you pick later are not nearly as good.

The Squirrel – He came, and his hiding place was under the eaves. He would jump from the apple tree over to the rain gutter. All winter he stayed there. Not so welcome in my cherry tree. The thief.

Art – Should I ever visit another country, I think I would choose Holland. To see Vermeer. It is very different from the empty art painted for the aristocrats of Italy and France. Vermeer was a true artist.

van Gogh's Letters – I have read much about art in recent years, but nothing has gripped me like van Gogh's letters to his brother Theo. This man's humility and motivation was deeply rooted in faith – not surprising that the Bible was his reading. Many knew more about art than van Gogh did, but his secret was to concentrate on what was real, what was core, and he stayed true unto death. It was this that demonstrated the depth of his honest character.

Buddha or Peace – (*Schon von Ferne fühlt der*) So deep and wonderful Rilke can be, so simple and clear. In his sonnet "Buddha," he has captured the wisdom and depth of Indian religion. Oh no, we know little of how much gold and how much jewelery needs to be melted to make a Buddha statue, but it is a lot.

And to achieve the treasured peace of spirit, your pride must be burned away, your desires relinquished, your will bent. Because there is a price that must be paid to achieve this great tranquillity.

Autumn 1952

Emerson – I re-read *Self-Reliance*. I see it is twenty-five years ago since I first read that essay, which is one of the bravest documents of modern literature.

It is a trial to face the creed of one's youth. For a creative artist – how much has one understood, how much has one veered from the path, does one have the same dedication? Lost one's course, lost one's way?

The Edda Poems – Incomparable! I think more and more highly of the *Elder Edda.* Yes, there are no other poems in the Norwegian literature that I hold more dear. This is our poetry. And the scholars agree that the wordsmith must have been from western Norway.

Evening – A blue summer evening. Dusk. Hedgehogs are rustling through the grass, grey night-moths fly hither and yon above the white clover and grass, softly against the night sky, floating and fluttering over the grass and red currant bushes still filled with unripe berries, and then they're gone like memories.

July, 1953

To Knotgrass

You're so small that no one sees you,
thoughtlessly they trod on you.
Truth be told, you act so humble,
scarcely calling for attention,
although I'm sure you shine for someone
huddled there by your grey rock.

A Westland River

Clutching a cleft
by the misty falls
ferns gather dew,
the river dances forth
cool and wild, rides
foamy white
over black boulders

and through empty weirs,
green-sheathed she toils
through deep dark pools,
then bright as a glacier spreads
by islets and sandy banks,
angry swirls tug
at fishing lines,
fence posts march into the water
and are gone –

Light – Recently, the electric company cut power for a week. As I entered the living room, smelling the paraffin and seeing shadows flickering softly and familiar in all corners, my childhood was suddenly vivid before me. Yes, this is very different from electric lighting. And candlelight is even cosier. And a burning sliver of pine even more so. They say this is progress.

And thus it is with the world as well. The most unpleasant oven of all is an electric one, whereas there is a wonderful sound from a wood-burning stove. And the hearth or fireplace is better yet.

When the Germans confiscated our radio, a divine peace settled in the house. People of culture try to live in the old ways the best they can: eating old-fashioned food, like cured meat and fermented trout, while sitting in old chairs.

Evening – He stood there in the evening, watching over the house. A home suddenly so dear. The old apple tree huddled by the wall of the living room, seeking shelter and warmth.

Loneliness – When I live in a house, I realize that I prefer to have the room that is farthest apart from the others. This yearning for solitude is great, but unfortunately it has been impossible for me to live alone. Yes, it is simply embarrassing to know that someone is in the next room. If they are further away, say in a room at the other end of the house, then it is much easier.

There is so much beauty in Rilke, such excellent sound, so much perfection; but isn't this overly sweet, like too much fragrance of myrrh and incense? Of well-tended gardens and cultivated people, of continental culture, flowering and decay? A bitter, bitter taste would be preferable to us working people. Mountain air.

Some Words – A blasting charge can shatter rock in many directions. A wheel may have many spokes. Goethe forgot this when he judged Hölderlin. His path was not Goethe's path, nor was it Schiller's; but Goethe writes as though there were no other path to Truth than the one he himself had walked.

September 1953

Been picking apples. A meager year. Not more than one thousand kroner for all my troubles. That's not much to live on. I hope next year will be better. I see new buds forming.

24 October

Went down to the village. It was quiet, with some fog. Raindrops and moisture on yellowed leaves. Autumn in Ulvik can be beautiful. Noticed that the bird-cherry by the church, with its black trunk and splayed branches, still held a few lemon-colored leaves in its crown. The bark of the bird-cherry is blacker than that of other trees.

Fog this evening, grey mountains protrude above it.

26 October

Mild, fine days. I lie in bed taking my afternoon rest. Sunlight between grey clouds. The top branches of the apple tree outside my window are naked, on other branches just a few yellow leaves. In the treetop it is still summer, lush and green, like the dark in greying hair – a few days of mercy. A bird flutters near the windowpane, sees reflected its own wings afire – you too will be coming!

27 October

Yesterday I drank at least ten cups of coffee, no wonder I am unwell today. And I went down to Brakanes to help Kårhild with some firewood. Brought up some dolomite for the fruit trees, packed two crates of apples. Even wrote a small poem while lying in bed during my afternoon rest. A small poem, almost Chinese. The Chinese say things so softly. We tend to reach for strong expressions when we write poetry, putting on a serious mask and making our voices deep. I suppose we have that from the bards of old, but it is not always needed.

Autumn is almost done for the year. The apple trees were somewhat later than the birch or rowan, and the leaves on the apple trees can be so beautiful. The cherry trees have a few leaves left, and swirl them about like red silken cloths.

3 November

Fine, light mornings. Lightly clouded, a slight wind, mild. The sky between the eastern clouds is matte enamel blue, the pines are silent and black, and the sea down there is sighing and blinking. Going out to cut wood to heat up water for washing today; the old poles that were used for drying hay will serve the purpose.

Wisdom – "Pay your respects to the spirits, but keep away from them. Strive instead to give people justice – that is wisdom!" – Confucius

Tao Te Ching – The texts of Lao Tzu are very strange. He is the giant amongst the Chinese sages. Since 1900 there has been a dramatic increase in the reading of Chinese literature in Europe, and all in all the influence of Eastern spirituality is perhaps the strongest force in modern European literature.

The strange thing is that many will gladly read Indian or Chinese religious works, while never opening a Christian book. It's hard to say why that is so. Routine, narrow-minded Christianity seems to have taken over Christian literature. Augustine and Eckhart and Pascal are now thrown into the same mental box as the itinerant fire-and-brimstone preachers.

Hospitality – Children are strange, they are so kind-hearted. I remember how I sat, waiting to see whether my family would offer visiting strangers food or drink. And when they did it pleased me; I was proud and happy on their behalf.

1955

Children and Animals – Children and animals know best who you are. They see not the outer person, but rather the inner man.

Hölderlin – On my last visit to Bergen I came across a little book of poems by Hölderlin. I had read only a few of his poems before, but immediately realized that this is one of the best poets I've read. Deep, sincere, a poet destined for posterity. Now I know him.

23 July

The Two Cognates of Chinese Thought - Yin and Yang. In my songs rules the Yin element, which stands for darkness, cold, weakness.

> I am the shady side,
> I am the Yin –
> How long shall it keep out
> the Yang from my nature?

5 February 1956

"When the heart weeps for what it has lost, the spirit laughs for what it has found." – *Sufi*

"The student learns by daily increment. The Way is gained by daily loss; loss upon loss until at last comes rest." – Lao Tzu

Tao Te Ching. The Way of Life by Lao Tzu. – It consists of eighty-one poems; one could call them modernistic, although I don't know their Chinese form. Nor do I know what the rules of Chinese poetry were two thousand years ago. But that is not the main point. If you can capture even some of the thought and spirit of them, there is much to be gained. For here is deep wisdom and great knowledge about life and humanity. In short: Lao Tzu is a mystic, and he has the same insight into the spiritual as we find in Eckhart, for instance. It is strange how much the great mystics resemble each other, even though thousands of years may separate them.

10 February

A New Page – A new page. Open and free, where you can really cavort. It's like discovering a mossy carpet in the forest as a child, a soft mossy carpet where you can do somersaults and tumble.

Much Reading – Too much reading suffocates the spirit. In the same way that too much manure will suffocate the roots of grass. No, Whitman was right.

13 March

Sunlight. Sunlight on white mountains and heavy snow. Yesterday evening the sky was starry and radiant; Orion with his raised bow was chasing the Pleiades, followed by Sirius passing Mount Grimsnut. That mountain appeared bluish, because of all the snow or the spring light.

These days I am out pruning trees. But I am careful, for I want branching. I am old enough to have seen fashions come and go when it comes to pruning. With fruit trees it's like with ladies' hats – one year it's supposed to be this way, another year that way. You shouldn't listen to everything you hear, not even to what the experts say.

Last Night – Last night I had the strangest dream ever. I remembered it well when I awoke, but as usual it soon unravelled like morning mist. I would, however, affirm this: however wild and meaningless dreams may seem, there is always meaning in them. I dreamt of becoming an animal, while still being a man – and knowing it. That's a trait of mental illness, too, that at one level you know that what you're imagining isn't right, but that you persist in it anyway.

A Good Gardener – A good gardener must be a mystic, otherwise he is no gardener.

Thoughts – Science has surely done a lot of good, increasing our knowledge considerably, but for millions of people it has also cut away the roots of life, i.e., taken away the mystical foundation of their life. Only the greatest souls have managed to unite science and mysticism, such as Goethe.

25 May
I am feeling emptier than I have for a long time. Neither a thought nor a poem occurs to me. Abandoned.

You might say that mystics and agnostics finally meet. It's not so strange that Eckhart was accused of being godless. You see it equally clearly in Simone Weil. It seems Kant's doctrine applies to mystics as well: even though there is no God… And Hindus and Taoists arrive at the same conclusion. No wonder Huxley refers to "the perennial philosophy".

Mystics, however, have always been great poets, and their writings are always enchanting.

A Cork – Your nature is like that of a cork, dancing easily and thoughtlessly on the waves as soon as the sinker stone no longer weighs you down. And the sinker stone is grief. It is grief that holds you upright, in your center, in your anchor-hold on life.

Sulking – As long as we are children, we sulk, wanting our mother and father. Later we sulk about fate and the way of the world.

Talent – If we never do more than what we can, it won't amount to much. We must do more than what we can.

Many people have no idea what poetry is; they think it a synonym of fantasy and illusion. Poetry is to concentrate or make denser, *verdichten* as the Germans say.

25 June
A bad poet only tears the web apart, whereas a great poet completes the web and waits for his prey.

1 July
It is always enjoyable to read poetry in a foreign language. The foreign and exotic is always enchanting. A foreign language is never as clear as your own, nor is it as worn. Everything, even the most ordinary thing, seems new.

21 July

Time-honored Weather Indicators – Today I'm sitting outside, writing. The cherry tree that stood outside my living room has grown so large that it casts a nice shadow. According to the weather forecast, there's a belt of rain clouds between Scotland and Iceland – and true enough, Mount Vassfjøra wears a cap of fog, which means rain is coming. It may not reach this far into the fjord, but that's another matter. This summer I have enjoyed comparing the old, time-honored weather indicators with the modern weather forecasts. It's fascinating how reliable those old indicators are.

30 July

The meadow at Løype appears grey and lush in the evening, luminous with flowering caraway here and there, which received a lot of rain this summer. A few clouds drift across the sky. Perhaps there's no rain coming, but certainly not good weather either. Balaona Falls still shines against the mountainside, there are still patches of snow up in the hollow there, it has more or less rained this summer.

31 July

The weather is unchanged. A drizzle in the mountains, none down here – but the clouds were probably emptied by then. Otherwise the weather is good. Mists are clinging far down the Sygnestveitlia hillside, the fjord appears strangely fresh and light blue. Perhaps it is more hopeful than the mountains; not even they know everything. However, the village appears lush and green after this rainy summer. Just look at the mountain pastures. This year they could have cut grass and ferns for fodder there.

10 August

This berry season is a dreadful time. Up at five in the morning to chase away birds. I put up a scarecrow the other day, but it's too old. I will have to be my own scarecrow.

22 November

When Will You Be Free? – When are you going to start writing poetry, in other words only the poems that inspire you, about that which is beautiful?

Steel

Will is steel.
Bare and blue.
Thus the steel remains
in a willed thought,
a willed feeling,
a willed deed.

Most beautiful is the thought
that foregoes steel,
most tender the feeling
that lacks it,
noblest the deed
that does without.

Will is our hidden steel,
our sharp edge against fate,
the lever that can pry
mountains aside.
But we do not like
to bare it.

It's play we love
and children and blossoms in the wind,
and we regard with awe
strong tides
and mountains that fall . . .

One Thing You Knew

One thing you knew:
the world's folly is a mountain
that withstood your onslaughts
and no one gave
more heed to
your words
than to the dog
across the fjord.

You wouldn't offer guidance
to anyone – only rage
against the mountain,
this brittle mountain
looms ever larger
until it's all
that's left.

When you noticed they started
listening to you,
you fell silent;
it can't have been
the hard granite
you'd touched.

You, who knew
the world's folly is
an icy sneering sword-proof mountain,
and that the way to wisdom
is endless!

Do the Next Man a Favor

He came down from
the mountains, heading home,
got himself ferried from Osa
out to Øydvinsto.
He was open-handed
and offered to pay.

But the man from Osa
would have none of it.
I want to pay
– I can't reach you
to return the favor.
Then do the next man
a favor,
said the man from Osa
and shoved off.

The Snowfield

Snowy winter and a cold spring.
Now Bumannen appears
again.

We had seen little sign of him,
just his shadow, a glittering helplessness
that shriveled and shrank,
until he hung there like the Seventh Master of the House
in a horn on the wall.
You need to know your way around these parts
to catch sight of him but
he's there all the same,
a remnant,
a shimmer.

This year he's back
full strength
– he basks in the sun on that barren mountain,
scouting after
his peers.

Seven Winds

Seven winds, seven winds
soughed and sang.
Seven winds, seven winds
found the heavens too small.

Seven winds, seven winds
clashed in gusts.
Their wild dance swirled,
tearing foam from the fjord!

Seven winds, seven winds
parted ways.
And today
all winds are still.

In the Hayfield

I came to a hayfield
one summer evening,
and on that hillside
I saw something.

Not a sprite in green dress
nor a ghost – no,
it was a far more
cheerful sight:

An old juniper and a foxglove
were in that fern-covered field.
With the foxglove leading
a tiny red-topped flock
by the hand,
and the juniper
leaning on its staff.

In the evening breeze they stood
in that meadow. Perhaps they meant
to go farther,
the foxglove and that juniper
and their little flock
– heading home
from the harvest
or moving elsewhere …

Troll

The troll in you
– that heavy, ugly shapeless thing –
wakes and stirs drowsily,
a blind grimace at the morning sun,
growls for food and ale.
Sated, that troll can be
rather good-natured,
peering at you
with a new wrinkle.
But not even a troll is
merely itself.

That troll in you
– you'll never make yourself
stifle that ugly beast. Instead
you echo others and laugh.
There's something quite familiar
and Norse about such trolls.
There is a shadow
in that ancient pine!

If you had the heart,
you could grip the axe
by the door – but you too would
fall into the grave.

Kin

If you're kin to the birch,
you'll last a long time,
endure both rain and wind,
and the field biting at your hair.
But you won't always be

bright and straight.
Birch rising from the scree
are knotted and gnarled
and with blackened twigs.

If you're kin to the pine,
you too will persist,
and the scrawnier your soil
the longer you'll last.
But your heartwood is brittle
and you're heavy in storm
and dour beneath the snow.

If you're kin to nard-grass,
you'll last the longest.
Splintery yellow, green-bearded,
full of rage and tough as hell.
Nothing bothers you
– and nobody wants you!

Show Us Your Field

Don't greet us with:
barking dog,
angry fist,
– keep off the crop!
But early one morning show us
your field of rye!

Launch the Boat

The sea tosses and turns in the darkness.
Launch the boat now?
Doubt and foreboding.
Yes, right now.
The night opens onto a vast space.
The sky has raised a wall to the west.
The moon appears, beaming –
Now it will happen.

The Cross

Third day of the wedding.
Drunk on the lively feast
and big event,
still in his bridegroom shirt at dawn,
he stumbled down
to the meadow by the shore,
to cut grass.

His scythe swung
a few times, before he stuck
the shaft into the ground,
spread out his arms
and lay down.

Boathouses and yellow gables
were mirrored in the water;
your shout would have echoed
between the mountains.

People busied with the harvest,
children climbing the cherry trees,
the scarecrow clapper rattling,
horses toiling and swinging
their tails at flies.

But on he slept.
He just lay there
on that meadow by the shore,
shining like a cross.

The River Across the Fjord

It falls and falls,
as it did yesterday,
falls from that cliff
where only eagles
soar –
ever falling,
falling hard
against the rockface
without a sound,
without song,
strives and falls
– gushes forth
from gorge and cleft
sprays
a frothy beard,
pauses,
hangs there
– falls
beyond time,
falls bound
in its nightmare
– can't get a word out,
not a sound . . .

The Crow

The crow is hardly an acrobat,
though she'll never cease trying.
See how she persists,
flapping her wings
to reach the forest!

Crows enjoy flying.
In the evening glow before the autumn storm
she strives to reach the hills.
Then she returns – soaring
in daring arcs
over the dark forests
and between the tree crowns,
like a youngster
eager and intoxicated.

The eagle is the master of flight,
the crow admits, and
solemnly moves her foot.
But she won't flee
when the eagle appears
above the mountains.

One day the crow saw a hen
flapping over the chicken-wire fence
and careen down.
You should have heard
that cackling hen
brag about flying!

The Seagull

You were a seagull,
and to think that
you would end like this!
While others take flight in the storm
you stand on a skerry screeching.

Hawk and Falcon

The falcon strikes,
feathers scatter in the air.
A claw-marked hawk struggles
to reach the river gorge.

The falcon rises,
still scouting.
Boldness was given wings
and bloodthirsty claws.

Reedgrass

A waterfall stumbles
down its cliffside,
the mountain shivers
above the sheltered valley.
The crag hangs its
green rag-rugs in the sun;
naked alder woods
hold their scattered harvest
of yellow willow leaves.
What does the shy
black thrush seek?
The lake below Lyse
grows ever darker.
By the estuary
reedgrass trembles,
empty seed-heads
bending toward shore.

Meeting

They met – uncertain
if they should greet each other.
But she spoke then, walked
a step or two alongside him.
We don't know
everyone after dark.
She was still young,
her gleaming eyes
just as black.

Words fell
like sinkers
from the sides of each boat,
with open sea between them.

Only afterward did he
notice they had tangled
somewhere in the depths,
where currents tug
over deep chasms and treacherous
kelp forests.

Wary she was.
How quick to break off!

But he held the end
of the broken line and her hook,
even if he didn't know
this was a lifeline
thrown to him.

Ghost

You're a ghost now.
A spirit.
And you circle
without clang or din,
having learned to
follow kin quietly
— stand like chaff
in the sunlight,
move softly as the moon
through the hayfield.
None know whether you
pass through their door;
where you tread
no animals are
startled.

You're a ghost now.
Concealed.
And if you are yourself
you're free.
It may pain us
to see doors open
and slam shut
– to see smiles stiffen
and masks fall
for our sakes.
Why should we
frighten the young?
A ghost should not
be heard nor seen.
Pass like the wind
with your words!

The Axehead

The old woodsman's axe
becomes downright sinister
on the whetstone.
The steel will spit
red rust,
sharp and hot,
when it's being ground.
But it'll scarcely chop wood
– it's all edge, maw.

Strange to be
a mere axehead,
this broad, hungry axehead,
instead of thick steel
hollow-cheeked
it's forced to trust
brittle iron.
This broad rust-pitted
axehead.

Sorry, I Thought

Sorry, I thought
that low fence would be
easy to jump,
  and I thought you might
  be grateful.

I realized
how foolish I
had been.
  But, truth be told, I am
  glad – and proud of you.

Slowly the Truth Dawns

To wake, and feel
your heart sinking
heavy and dark,
hardening …

Slowly the ocean lifts its wave,
slowly the woods redden in the gorge,
slowly the fire licks the logs in hell,
slowly the truth dawns …

Korea

Side by side. Enemy and friend, grass now grows
between your ribs and poppies glow
in hollow eyes; rusted weapons weep
till all is forgotten beneath brush and grove.

Now you're at peace. It no longer concerns you
where the border lies; neither right nor wrong
was victor here. Death's insight soars above teeth
strewn by years, warring over lines on a map.

I see you, bone-men of Korea's soil, ghosts
cast shadows behind the peace table talks – your death,
brother, was but the planned offal of valor.

Death has no words, only this pale grin
by leaders of cold conscience. Your sentence
stamped and signed – put away, forgotten.

There Is Still Time

You sing for
old shadows,
shadows of
yourself.

Unborn visions
threaten your day
– when will you
give them life?

You think
there's still time
– the grass is
still green.

Spring Seas

There's something sinister in his gift,
something strange and grim
in the glass-green growth
this spring sun will not accept:
a green grown in another world.
There's a scent of rotten silt, a whiff
of sludge and slimy stones and
seaweed tangle rising from
those black depths.

It's true enough – that velvet green border
he tries to gift these naked shores
was woven under ice; he knows
they've long since had
grass and buttercups.

But in the dusk his compassion
glows soft green, his velvet edge around
these frozen lands. And the weaver
warily withdraws and shuts
his eye.

The Golden Cock

I was long dead. Dead inside my shell,
and I crowed like the golden cock of Constantinople.
I lived below – heard rasping and response
and resisted – the hollow sound of sold souls.

Until the dream shook me awake one festive yellow night,
my disguise fell, and all the glitter turned to dust.
I am home, at the threshold. The house is asleep
and suddenly this child's heart is beating joyously again.

I stand with my hand on the latch to my mother
and father's room – the moon is shining on worn floorboards.
"You've been gone so long?" it comes, without words.

From beyond the room, grief sounds its heavy clapper.
Then the dream releases me. In my golden belt
I once more crowed for the Emperor and swore.

Luminous Spaces

Sacred star!
Coldly you spread
luminous spaces
– cold radiance.

Your one great experience
also unfolds
luminous spaces
that guard
the core of
light.

Don't come near,
never too near!
There shall be
luminous spaces
between all things
until the end of time.

On the Eagle's Perch

På ørnetuva

1961

Overleaf: On his farm in Ulvik, Hauge tended roughly two hundred trees – not the dwarves that the fruit farmers of Hardanger plant today, but hardy decent-sized trees, many of which were heritage apples.

One day, Hauge reported the discovery of strangely reddish apples that were hanging on a branch in the crown of one of his neighbor's Prince trees. Conferring with his mentors Per Stedje and Prof. Bjarne Ljones, Hauge suggested naming this apple *Edling*, meaning "the noble one," while echoing the pronunciation of the farmer's name, Erling-Ola, in his local dialect. (Archives of the Olav H. Hauge Centre, Ulvik, Norway.)

Excerpts from Hauge's Journals – through autumn 1961

10 January 1957

Modernism – That's the latest literary fashion in this country. Well, it's not so new. It seems to me that much of the literature that bears this label is rather nebulous, but I suppose new stars may form in a nebula, this time as well. Some poems are a storm, or "a rush and a tide" as Swinburne would say. Some are clear as crystal or dewdrops, like Emily Dickinson's. Others are mountains of thought like those of Browning. And yet all are wondrous and great, proving that poetry can be many things.

What characterizes T.S. Eliot, of whom I am very fond, is his always conscious, alert style. He is always searching, always trying, always weighing and considering, often stuttering or fumbling after the right word. *That* I like. He never falls back into habit, to "the rifling of rooves" as Browning put it. The same quality distinguishes his prose. Eliot's style is never slick, and that is why he is not easy. It comes as no surprise that in his youth he was heavily inspired by Browning.

15 February

Chaucer was no fool. He understood people and forgave them their weaknesses and faults. But he never forgave arrogance.

A Thought on Poetry – This game is when the image rises from the depths into the light, like an air bubble – that is part of the secret of poetry.

Modernism – They are greedy, these modernists. As soon as a poet achieves something, they claim him as a modernist. Well, I agree with them, and a lot of excellent verse carries that label. Shall we define it? Complete freedom, images and symbols used freely, ordinary rules of logic no longer apply; the new poetry is no more bound by law than is a dream.

Solitude – The hermit must be a strange man. You say he's afraid of people. Often he is, but often there is no one who loves humanity more than him, no one who understands people better.

Play – Play the instrument you have. Nobody says you have a Stradivarius at hand. (After reading about stylistic theory)

Madness – Is most often an intensity of emotion and imagination, so that you forget yourself. The inner world becomes the only real one.

Burdened – Constantly burdened, in the dark, dispirited and depressed, unfree, never a happy heart! Such is my life. Simone Weil speaks so much about "*la pesanteur*," the gravity that pulls you down under. You have slaved away so long that you can't handle grace, or "bliss" as I would call it.

For grace is true freedom, and something different from the blind rapture I have experienced. To experience grace and still be human, must be a great thing. "*Deux forces règnent sur l'universe: lumière et pesanteur*," says Simone Weil. (Two forces rule our universe: light and gravity.) So far I am only familiar with gravity. My world is grey.

Ten Hectares of Land – Arne Garborg desired – according to his diary – to own ten hectares of land and to be a free man. Then he would not have to toil and write for a living. Yes, free. Well, Garborg had little idea what he was saying.

28 May

Beautifully sunny weather these days. The orchards are in bloom. I have never seen it this lush and green during the blossoming. Yesterday evening I sat gazing at a Säftaholm apple tree. Such lively green leaves, such radiant white flowers against the snow-covered mountains.

A word by Thomas à Kempis: "Blessed indeed be the ears that heed what God speaketh and teacheth inwardly in the soul."

8 June

The greatest tragedy that can happen is to be shut out from that hidden room within us. It can happen, you know. The door can close. Or we can become so busy with our outer lives that we forget about this room. It may also be that it becomes sad and squalid in there. If so, then it is our own fault that we do not manage to create something new there, to conjure forth that magical world that once enchanted us.

The Eye of Your Soul – "Love looks not with the eyes, but with the mind," it says in *A Midsummer Night's Dream,* and it is true. What says the artist; should he not always be seeing with the eye of his soul? Indeed, he should. Most people, however, have "too much business with the passing hour," as Yeats puts it, or they are "caught in that sensual music," as he writes elsewhere. That is what sin is.

Whitman's View of the Poet – In one of the first small poems in *Leaves of Grass* is a line that reveals much about Whitman's view of his own poetry. In "Shut not your doors," he writes: "The words of my book nothing, the drift of it everything."

It is the pulse, the underlying current in his poetry, that captures our imagination. And that tells us: here is a great soul, a man with a great heart.

13 October

Here I shall merely make an observation of things I have thought about a long time. There are three kinds of poems:

1. Poems of this side, seen through ordinary eyes.
2. Poems at the boundary, where the light from the other side breaks through and visions are revealed.
3. Poems of the other side. Rarely, if ever written.

Strengthening – It is strange how good books strengthen us, indeed it is necessary to read great authors to keep the mind healthy. Last night I felt a little heavy and distracted. After reading some Coleridge I went to bed calm and with a focused mind. I have not yet immersed myself in all the wise and wonderful things he says about Shakespeare, but I shall.

Listen for Poetry – "Pound has lent ear to poetry." That's right, listen for the poetry; that's exactly what you should be doing. It may be found in so many places.

The Great Cultus – Heraclitus left hardly anything behind – at least not as far as we know – but it is enough for us to realize he was wise. There is something about him that reminds me of Lao Tzu. Many have been fascinated by the hidden, powerful utterances that we do know, amongst them Hölderlin and later Nietzsche.

Rhetoric – Follow all the rules of rhetoric, and you will get a well-ordered day out of your poem.

Silken Web

The poet weaves his silken web,
weaves his dream roses
fair and enchanting,
lures his reader – while
he himself sits hidden,
guarding his web
and prey.

14 January 1958
One day I started reading the *Book of Job*. Great literature. There is a lot of poetry in Job, the greatest novel of that age.

18 January
Snow – Yesterday it snowed all day. Today it is cold, everything is covered in half a meter of snow. I need to clear the paths around the house, and shovel the snow from the road all the way up to Øvregardsveien. I make this proverb on the model of Solomon: "Clear the snow from the road to your house, lest your guest pass it by!"

A Poem is a Universe – A poem is a universe: final, but still boundless, built up according to the same laws: harmony but also strife; tranquillity but also unease; at rest but also en route; reality but also dream; lie but also truth.

A poem should not be thick, dead substance. Rather it must have light and the space between worlds – and the more tension is there, the more it inspires your thoughts to leap. Words are worlds, and a poem's images are its constellations.

Give Me Working People! –That's the good thing about the smallholders and farmers of western Norway – they're just as they seem. They toil and struggle for themselves and their family. There are taxes to be paid, bad times to be survived, buildings to be repaired or built, livestock to be raised and bought, they and their children need clothes – and the kids need schooling when they're old enough. This is why the westland farmer is a striver, and neither with words nor deeds does he hide that. He must be thus, if he wants to live. Often he understands that it's wrong to be so absorbed by his daily toil; he might wish to read and learn, to get a wider perspective.

But consider the people who have fought their way up to a better life and more free time, such as clerks and teachers and what not, what are they thinking about? This is something I have often had the chance to notice. They think about having a good time, a pleasant and relaxing time; how to decorate their houses, what to wear and what to eat. They need a car, a cabin in the mountains, a boat, a camera, a cassette recorder, a refrigerator and more. Their thoughts go no further than that. They are no longer creative, for they only play at work so as to collect their wage. Their time goes on get-togethers and playing bridge. I far prefer the farmer! He still lives in striving, even if for nothing else than his daily bread.

Two Psychologists – There are two psychologists who are worth reading: William James and Jung. The others are mere nonsense. There might, however, be much to learn from parapsychology, as a supplement. Jung's philosophy is very interesting, but so are the new horizons opened by parapsychology. In short, there is nothing new in all of this, only an affirmation of established common sense and savvy, which is never to be despised. But it is so strange to see it presented in a scientific language.

Sun Worship – A letter from the Bergen Historical Museum. I had written telling them of the sacrificial pits I had found at Seberg.

Yes, worshipping the sun was not a stupid religion! Perhaps the most important. Strange how everything changes. The old ones must have understood that the sun was the giver of life, all life on earth. The sustainer. Without the sun there would be neither earth nor consciousness here.

And Death Shall Have No Dominion – I have never written – not even in my diary – of my experiences at Nevengården and Valen, altogether five years. Here I shall only mention that during those years, however much my condition and moods changed, one thing was certain: *There was no death.* Everything had been and would continue to be. Change, growth and diminishment were natural, while death such as we usually understood it did not exist. Should the thought occur to me – and I know it did, for I remember what I used to think about – it was with great sadness and pain. That was the strange thing, that whenever I recalled the time I had lived, from childhood onward, my work, life as a young man and such, it always hurt. It was a smaller and sadder time, a sorry condition from which I had been lifted into a higher home.

I shall try to remember the various things I experienced during those years, but first of all I have not had the courage to do so, and not because it hurts to recall those years – quite the contrary – but because we tend not to speak of our most valuable experiences.

10 November

A clear, sunny day. Snow stretches halfway down the hillside. Leaves are swaying in the sun, those that are left. Fruit trees hold onto their leaves longest, and they are like sparkling bouquets of fire throughout the village. That is the orchards. The deciduous forest is black, sprinkled with snow.

You May Not See It Yet but you should be certain that you're doing the right thing when you're following your innermost impulse and the best in yourself, and this you shall never regret. The innermost and best is – God. In the hour of your greatest need you will realize that. At that moment all else pales into insignificance.

My Poems are ordinary. Grey, heavy. In other words not imbued with the life of "Poetic Genius" of which Blake speaks. His are filled with light and life, and they seem effortless. I am still busy laying bricks in the basement, working below ground. I can only dream of the house above.

5 December

Even a crow becomes a sun-bird with golden wings when it flies into the joyous sunlight.

It Wasn't in Darkness – It wasn't in darkness that I lost my way, but in daylight. In darkness – for I have been there, too – I once again saw the stars.

Another Plane, in Another Dimension – The poetic genius should move in dimension that is distinct from our ordinary senses. However, when it takes the lead, to others it may appear as though you lose control. That was my misfortune. Suddenly the spirits pulled me up short, and I became confused, or got bats in the belfry as our forefathers said. I entered another home, a home of madness, that is the only explanation I can give you.

The radiance and views there, the journeys between worlds, the voices and ecstasy, it all made me dizzy. It was more than I could stand. That's why I am hesitant to speak of that adventure. It was overwhelming! So terrible that I think most who have experienced it fall silent. "*Jeder Engel ist schrecklich*," writes Rilke, and means what he says. Bliss might well be beyond our comprehension, but it is still a frightening thing. To be now in Eden, now in Valhalla, now a breath, now like some creature under the earth, now carrying dead animals – they too exist.

To journey between worlds is common, to visit distant abodes of the gods.

Without a Compass – Many wander the earth, and through heaven and hell, but do they have a compass? That is the question.

Poetry without Dream is nothing. But modern poetry is a theoretical dream, a willed dream, a manufactured dream.

Gazing Out Over the Fields This Spring Day – The sap rises in trees and bushes everywhere, call it the creative, nurturing force. Thus also the spirit rises in people and animals – creative and nurturing life – for everyone. Each of us is only a shell, a fragment, a spirit in eternity...

Like Crossing the Stream to Fetch Water – If you have understood what the old sages meant by "it" when they said, in ordinary language, "it grows," "it is apparent," then you are close to comprehending Plato and Emerson.

Accept the language of the old sages, for there is much insight and experience therein, and none express it better. Those who made this were greater poets than you are.

I belong to those wretched people who need to read books to keep on an even keel.

Thought and dream are heavenly vehicles.

20 March 1959

Eccentrics and Misfits – Most often they're people who listen more to their heart or conscience than they do to convention or other people.

Making poetry is humility. Blessed be the poet who takes the time to remain for a while in his poem; that's what I miss most of all today.

The truths in this world are few and simple. You don't have to go searching high and low for them. You don't even need to read all the books.

The world would be a better place if there weren't so many people who insist on enlightening others. They don't believe Our Lord gave anyone but them eyes and ears, let alone wisdom. Those who intruded into my life in order to enlighten and guide me, they only did damage. Leave people in peace!

Our curse is that we demand silver of this world, without knowing it would give us gold. You don't know what might bring peace to your fellow human being, even though you might think you know. Do not pull the harrow too often across your field, to remove the weeds you see. A thought can give you wings, but also drag you down like a stone. Knowledge is easy to carry, but a thought is either a stone or wings.

Why all this strife? Find yourself a branch on the tree of life, find bliss under the sun, find storm in the embrace of eternity!

There are branches and snags in life. Those who wish to climb will find them. It's no use to point them out to someone else, from above or from below! Speak of what you see – you who are above; voice your lament if you are left below! That should do.

The Greatest Experience of My Life – "Diamonds are moments. The Language of Salvation." –Henrik Wergeland

Our spirit is made of a stronger substance than all others. Spirit is more akin to a diamond than anything else I know. That is why poetry is the act of concentrating rather than dispersion (of light, air, waves).

We are like croquet balls, lie still on the ground until the mallet whacks us. There is will behind that mallet. We're to go through that gate, but we're hardly willing. The path is clear. And there is that mallet again. One solid whack. A will. We must go. There.

I have a window facing west, high on the wall of my living room. In the evening a star appears there; the spring evenings are so light and blue. I recall the stars of my youth, they didn't shine in the sky, but rather in my soul I thought, so large and high and trembling. Now the star appears in the sky, and I must be content with that. That, too, is beautiful.

5 April

The smell of manure and new green grass, isn't that a joyous sign of spring? And isn't that the smell of spring that someone who has grown up on a farm remembers best?

7 April

Fine weather, sunny. It looks like early spring this year. The ice has broken long ago; usually it doesn't retreat from shore until the 14th of April, or disappear entirely until the 25th of April. The snow is retreating, although there are still a few white patches on Kongsberg. Kvasshovden is towering dazzling white above Bergahaugane. It's a beautiful morning. The hillsides are turning green, and the sun and wind are embracing. A few crows are building nests up in Løypet, that's early for crows. On Bergaberget, the milk truck is chugging uphill.

12 April

For a long time I will be enjoying *Walden* by Thoreau. True enough, what he has to say is neither exciting nor adventurous. He doesn't brag or encounter much. I don't know whether he sees otters or woodchucks; goose and tawny owls are probably the largest birds. No, clearly the swallow, squirrel, hawk and other ordinary creatures are interesting enough for him. The forests here are pretty much like those in Concord. He's never seen moose or bear. A good disciple of Zen.

Poetry – Not the white light itself, but in the light of the white light.
Not the one, but both – united.

Life is Suffering – If you cannot accept this truth, then you will never understand anything. Never grow, never rise high, never amount to anything.

The Days – No one has written about the days that come "muffled and dumb like barefoot dervishes," as Emerson has. Take "Days" for example. If this is not a poet, then I don't know who is! I think of Zen.

Christmas Humphreys' writing on Zen in *Buddhism* is admirably clear. Just look at pg. 181.

One Thing is Needed – The artist needs to have a creative imagination – all the rest comes of its own accord when you work.

Without creative imagination the details of your work will fall apart.

But is creative imagination an ability one can train and use wilfully? That depends. Probably not. Yet still: maybe. Remember what Gustaf Fröding writes in *Prince Aladdin of the Lamp*: "Without the ring you are not much worth."

Creative imagination is a precious ability, which should have all means placed at its disposal.

Prince Aladdin of the Lamp – recall Baudelaire's and Coleridge's view of the creative enterprise. Or creative wonder, as I would call it.

6 May

Today I had to light the stove, that's how cold it was. Now it's snowing on the cherry blossoms.

The weather is miserable, cold and wet. I have been reading Baudelaire, as best I can with my limited French. Time to go out and graft a few apple trees.

Snow in May on the grass and yellow buttercups.

29 May
These past few days I have been reading a fascinating book again and again, which I got in 1954. It's David Stafford-Clark's *Psychiatry Today.* I have tried my hand at what the author calls "mental illness," so it's interesting to see how the experts define it. I suppose that's a little useful. God only knows? I happen to believe that what a psychiatrist may call "mental illness" is often the highest order of mental health. But one had better keep such thoughts to oneself.

20 June
If you are rich enough to hear the wind sighing in the leaves at dusk on a grey summer evening – then there is still hope for you.

24 July
The will desires one thing, the heart another – and which is right? Would someone answer me that riddle.

I realize that the path I have started won't lead me where I want to go; and yes, it is leading me astray. Nevertheless I must follow that path, for I am not done with it, I have not reached its end. I must see where it leads; only then can I abandon it.

Many authors have managed to write the equivalent of several bibles. I can't fathom that they can have done much else. When did they read? When did they reflect? When have they walked through the fields listening to the wind? And when could they possibly have spent time with others? Perhaps it is the quill that did their thinking for them, it's amazing how it can be trained.

25 July
It's getting dry. Sunny and windy, day after day. Many apples are dropping, and they are small. The cherries are almost harvested. Quite a toil. I thought I might be able to get away soon, but there's no chance of a trip now!

It doesn't take great language skills before one poet is able to read the works of another. It is as though an old hunter is following tracks through fresh snow.

A Countryman of Ibsen – "A countryman of Ibsen had really no need of external inspiration," says Herbert Read of Edvard Munch (*Philosophy of Modern Art*). There is more truth to that than we realize. Do we Scandinavians really have that much to learn from the Continent or Britain? I only ask.

Even Socrates the intellectual offers a comment on Dionysian wisdom. In *Ion* he speaks of the poet.

The Romanticist cultivates the creative, the sprouting seeds – the Classicist cultivates form.

Naturalism in Art corresponds to a certain level of consciousness, the ordinary view of life, which is the view to which ordinary decent people aspire.

Few Reflect on This – Eliot says that "his poetry, Dante's, is one of those which one can only just hope to grow up to at the end of life." Those are wise words. Few of us consider this when examining great works of art: that we must grow in order to understand, and that we may not yet be ready to comprehend.

14 August

It's still hot and dry. Wasps are eating up the plums. The apples are losing their grip and falling from the trees. Rain!

15 August

Last night there was a good shower, the rain came splashing down for a while. But then the wind picked up again, a hot wind, and it was hardly possible to sleep. I am writing this at four-thirty am. It's morning but no longer light. The year is already getting old.

21 August

The good weather continues. Started reading R.Cl. d'Oullins. I picked and packed one hundred kg of apples today. I also try to get some reading done, even though plenty of tasks remain. I'm making a humble effort to continue my studies, especially of Emerson. Hadn't read *Representative Men* before. That's exactly what it is, you should never let the world gain the upper hand. Even when Goethe was on the battlefield, he would turn his attention to his color theory in the evening; he didn't let the turmoil of war disturb him. Good old Schopenhauer underscored this; to me it is a fine example of perseverance and maintaining one's mental equilibrium. Most people are slaves to their emotions, and they take them all too seriously.

I would rather see a healthy barbaric revolt against "prudence" – the polished exteriors and uptight attitudes of the petit-bourgeoisie – they're like athletes with ramrod backs.

Differences – Tourists are wandering about every which way. I came across two English ladies, just now, who had strayed into the orchard. Not that they had done anything wrong, not at all, but I went out and had a word with them. They told me they were looking for a bench with a view, as though this were public property. I pointed out that my neighbor Nils had a garden bench at the edge of the hill – but that it was on private property. They were a little startled when I mentioned private property; it hadn't occurred to them that anything in Norway might be private, and that they couldn't just wander and sit where they pleased. Then they told me that in England no one was allowed to set their foot on private land, that there were notices with *Trespassers will be Prosecuted* everywhere.

3 October

Tomorrow I shall harvest the potatoes, the weather forecast is good. I still have the Cox Pomona and Laxton's Superb apples left to pick. Then I have to label and take the trouble of delivering the crates. Finally things will settle down a bit and I will have more time. It's been awfully busy lately.

30 October

This is the autumn of autumns! I have never seen the foliage more beautiful. The leaves of the pear trees along the fjord are brick-red; I've never seen them thus. Apples and other trees are yellow, as usual. Snow-topped mountains. Smoke rises from the house on the wharf; someone is still taking the trouble to bake in the old way, bread and pastries.

This Hardanger! Vassfjøro, Onen, Hårteigen, Oksen – each of these mountains stands alone, weathered and streaky, silently familiar with each other, at least once the tourists have left!
Whoever carries a grief is not homeless.

A poem may be like a breezy summer day, or like shady woods or the calmly breathing sea; but there are also poems that are pliant as grass in the autumn sun, as dark and silent and shut as mountains; I especially like the latter. Should my memories last, I may return and beat on the walls of those crags.

15 November

Tonight I watched Tolstoy's *War and Peace*. A spectacular film. Magnificent. And Audrey Hepburn is peerless.

What is the Matter? – Modernist poems are like a field of weeds sprayed with a hormone-based herbicide – artificial, unnatural plants that grow themselves to death.

Many great truths have been abandoned; they stand there staring at us, smiling. Now the same fate is threatening the greatest of all truths.

The wind, brother and sister, play across the hillsides – hand in hand, dancing, pausing, whispering secrets and casting silken scarves to each other.

20 November

It's as hard work to be immoral as it is to be virtuous.

We find life wears on us and grinds us like a river stone, and unfortunately it is the hardest in us that remains.

Don't struggle against solitude, but embrace it as the gift it is.

Poet – there's the question of how you travel. This is your choice, not an ability. Some prefer to proceed on foot, being distrustful of broom or Eastern carpet.

Poems are formed not in broad daylight, but under your blankets. Remember the old sagas; the Viking bard Egil Skallagrímsson would crawl under his sheepskin when he wished to make verse. Only that which rises as an image before your inner eye is worth writing about.

That's why Hölderlin and Novalis and Goethe, Emerson and Ewald are smiling; they had gained insight into the spiritual realm.

The One Who Suffers Greatly - Misfortune always leads to reality congealing and hardening, physically speaking, into a harder and more bitter reality. Even time becomes material, matter, something you can touch and sense. You need to have suffered to understand that. That's why you find bitterness and hardness in such people. I have been there myself. Simone Weil understood that and wrote insightfully of this. You especially see this in people who are shut away in prison or insane asylums. But there are also those who are victorious in the face of such circumstances; and, yes, it is precisely amongst these people we find those who are most liberated. This is proof of the spirit's omnipotence.

15 January 1960
The ground is frozen. I worry about my apples, they must not freeze! I hope all goes well! Snow!

The Dewdrop and the Snowflake – For a long time, thunder and sunsets were the models for poetry. A poem was supposed to be like a storm – salty and invigorating, going to the root, but also breezy; or it should be as moving as a sunset. Later the dewdrop became the ideal; it was a tiny world unto itself, which in a trembling, bursting *now* mirrored the universe. Today it is instead the snowflake that is our model: this miraculous galaxy of ice crystals that seems a revelation of nature's very pattern of beauty, and which humankind cannot hope to imitate, even with our greatest efforts.

It Is Time – The life of a soul has different phases. There is a time to grow, to love, to let go, to shine; there is a time to pull yourself together, to withdraw, to barricade yourself; there is a time to sleep, perhaps for eternities.

The Hidden Path —What is it that allows us to visit the realm beyond? Impossible to say. It happened to me last night, and by the way, it has been a long time. I was in the Beyond again, where everything is different.

I don't know, but it is heavenly, otherworldly. This time I arrived there in a peculiar way, in a vehicle or some such thing that ran on electricity. I just got on it, pressed some buttons – and then I was in the Beyond.

It is the way, how to get there, that is the question that no doubt has stumped so many people. The way. Here, we can't help feeling that we have lost something, a key or something vital. (Our yearning to speed along in a car or plane may be come as a result of this, our yearning after that realm which most people know something of, because often they arrive there by flight.) I myself have experienced that this transition, from ordinary consciousness to this other awareness, happens when I am ill. It was especially common during my time at Valen Mental Hospital, and it would happen both night and day, or during various kinds of turbulence, but how and why? Many people have no doubt pondered this question, and that is the path the mystic seeks – and probably finds. (What passes for "mysticism" today, has nothing to do with what I mean. Some hidden insight, a liberating experience, or some momentary relief through contemplation seems sufficient for them.)

A Classic —A classic is never difficult. It is like fine wine: clear and well-aged.

23 February

The morning sky is blue as a bell when I get up, and it is very striking before I turn on the lights. To the west, the moon floats beyond the black branches of the cherry tree, one edge grey and blurry, but its nail is luminous and hard. I think of Novalis and his "Blaue Blume" (Blue Flower).

Someone who writes little always has a sharp pencil.

That they are unable to see the meaning of nature is one thing, but to be unable to see any meaning in their life is to deny what is human in us.

It is the heartbeat that dictates the words, lines and rhythm of a good poet, and not the rules of grammar or rhetoric – or exactly those, at their very best.

22 March

Today I awakened and I was awake. Everything was somehow opened. The birds and everything alive, yes, even the dead, knew all about each other and were listening and answering; even the flies, and the seagulls that came and sat on my hand. Well, this is nothing new; I have experienced such things often, and not only in dreams. But then you get up and start your day, and reality settles down again, or retreats in a way, although not quite as solid and grey as before.

28 March

I have been reading in Goethe *erzählt sein Leben*. It really is a fine book. At first a letter from the author or one of his acquaintances, then comes a poem, then excerpts from his other writings. He uses everything as a point of departure: stones and animals and plants, the barometer (Eckermann points out that he talks about Nature's inhalation and exhalation), colors, light, art, literature, mining. It may have been that his science was relatively simple (the theories were many and complex, but the facts were few), nonetheless, he would have grasped the core challenges of our day as well.

Always and forever the same. What are you cultivating? Time or eternity – to which do you belong? Lust or love?

Hemingway – I give him as an example of a modern writer – had great insight into people's physical and instinctive reactions, but he knew nothing about the laws of the spirit. Shakespeare had the same knowledge Hemingway did, but he also had that other insight. Without it he would not have been Shakespeare.

Why shouldn't Shakespeare or Goethe be just as worthy guides as Freud and Hemingway? Oh, you fools! But when you believe in Kinsey, well. Has Kinsey ever interviewed a Romeo or a Juliet? A thousand utterances from ordinary people, but should we be compelled to model our lives after them?

There is old earth in Rilke, old monasteries and churches, old vineyards and rose gardens, old parks and castles, where much is wizened or rotted. If you have the time and patience to follow his convoluted thinking, then that is good.

Work and Pray! – Greater words have not been uttered, and they are of value even if you are toiling with worldly things. This work too has its rewards.

Watched Hemingway's *The Old Man and the Sea*. Yes, how many understood that film? He dared to sail too far out. And the sharks. Everything is there. The man who ventures too far out. And who manages to hook a great marlin and will not yield. And the sharks that smell blood. They are here. An allegory. Yes, he knows how to do this.

You don't lay plans for a great poem, because what your intellect is capable of amounts to so little. A greater hand is needed, an eye that sees deeper than yours.

I never call myself a poet. It's so rare I am one. Most often I am an ordinary man.

Speak for yourself, and you will speak for everyone.

On Madness – G.K. Chesterton's essay on madness is wonderful! I should read it again every morning! See Blake!

Fragments of a Diary is confessional writing, a testimony by the author. It is strange that the development he describes is by and large similar to that of religious development. His corridor corresponds to "The Way" of Lao Tzu, and which we also find in the *Bhagavad-Gita*, Saint Teresa, Thomas à Kempis; the only difference is the words used.

Our life needs heaven and hell, lest it rot.

11 May

The cherry trees are blossoming. In the evening, hundreds of bumblebees can be heard in the treetops. And there is one sunny day after another, warm as though it was summer.

The cherry tree stood naked and black in the winter. Now it rests its chin against the evening breeze, swaying gently with its dazzling white flowers.

17 May

Splendid weather. It pains me that I sprayed the trees with insecticide last Friday, after all the blossoms had opened. Now I see bumblebees staggering half-dead through the door; it's not nice to kill your best friends of the orchard. It didn't occur to me that the dandelions were in full flower; the poison settled there, too.

Sprayed poison, then went inside to read Emily Dickinson and Dorothy Wordsworth; how heartless and perverted can I be!

Emily and Dorothy, they are somewhat related, and perhaps I should mention Emily Brontë as well, there we have three strange female authors of English literature. Strange that Dorothy Wordsworth isn't mentioned by Louis Cazamian.

Two bumblebees staggered through the door, unable to fly, and lay down to die – as if accusingly. It is easy to see that this is death by DDT. I found two more dead beneath an apple tree. Tragic. How thoughtless I was!

19 May

Bad headache all day, unable to read.

Common people and poor people have the most beautiful headstones. They are at least simple and make no demands.

No, I must heed this headache. Otherwise I may again be unable to read and write, which I was for many years.

What would I do if I didn't have books to turn to? Emily Dickinson writes:

"Unto my books so good to turn
Far ends of tired days,"

She knew how to appreciate her little book collection. She talks about "kinsmen of the shelf."

Today I spoke with this year's first tourist, an American lady walking down from the upper farms. A small, skinny and energetic lady, with glasses and inquisitive eyes. I happen to mention that it was rare to see American travelers wandering on foot. "I have not come the long way from Chicago to Norway to sit in the hotel room smoking and drinking, playing cards," she said. "I want to enjoy nature and the country."

23 May

Read the sixteenth chapter of the *Iliad,* about Patroclus who fell into the king's coat of mail, as Hölderlin puts it in "Mnemosyne." Magnificent descriptions! And most instructive writing. If you have good fortune, you must beware of hubris, arrogance; that will be your downfall.

2 June

Finished the *Iliad.* Spent exactly one month reading that and the *Odyssey*. I have no regrets, even though I can't help thinking how I might have experienced reading it at fourteen! The desire to swing the sword and grab the spear is deeply entrenched in us all! Snorri Sturluson is bad, Homer is worse.

Enlightenment today: knowing what model car and which brand of refrigerator your neighbor has.

I run into English housewives along the road; sometimes they speak to me. For the most part they want to know what we eat and drink, how we prepare our food, how many rooms we have in our houses, whether the children have to go to school, etc. It's the sphere of interest defined by *Woman's Day*. One lady asked me about my beliefs, but she was from Chicago, poor dear, and she believed in something as old-fashioned as God and the Bible.

Whitsun. 5 June

These words of Kierkegaard should provide solace for bachelors:

"Or has anyone ever heard of any man having become a poet through his wife?"

25 June

Yes, it has been taken from you. The orchard looked so good, rarely have I seen the apple orchard looking better. But one evening thunder-clouds rolled across the village, unleashing hailstones large as bird-eggs. Sharp, shiny ice – I've never seen the like. They danced like rocks against the road. Obviously there's scarcely an unbruised apple left on the trees.

30 June

– A thousand tasks need doing. Received crates today, stowed them in the barn loft. The berries are ripening. The birds are bothersome. I should be thinning some of the apples. And I should lacquer some of the floors. I should be spraying, too; there may be some fruit that is still salable after the hail did its damage. And the shopping and cooking need to be done. No, I am a slave.

2 July

Cold. Northerly wind. Up at four a.m., chasing away birds. A desolate summer morning, the wind bears tidings of autumn. The mountains are naked, most of the snow has been scraped away. An autumn wind through the green landscape. There's a loneliness in the room. Something has left. I notice it even in the cool grey kitchen. Something has left. Gone.

21 August

On Saturday I proofread my poems for the anthology Samlaget is publishing this autumn. The poems – twenty in all – don't look too bad.

Autumn is on the way. The plums are ripening. No, I have too much to do, too many wearisome tasks large and small. I learned nothing in my youth, I see that now. There was only work, early as well as late. Work at home, work for others. I should have learned something then. My reading was haphazard; for the most part I devoured whatever I came across.

10 September

Bought provisions. Washed the floors and tidied the house. No fruit picking today.

Surrendering to religion is to surrender oneself to grief over the imperfection of life and to our deeper yearning for something greater and better.

8 October

The hillsides across the fjord are as yellowish-brown as a bearskin. The fields are dotted with birches crowned with yellow leaves, surrounded by the dull steel of conifers; the cultivated fields are shiny green below grey mountains, the sky is dark and looming. Autumn. I am so busy that I haven't had time to notice it before.

The great solitary geniuses. The history of American literature is the story of great solitary geniuses. Hawthorne, Emerson, Thoreau, Poe, Melville, Whitman, Twain, Dickinson, all of them were solitary, distinct and different.

27 October

A can of pears, that's good enough. While they were cooking, I read Mauriac: *Mémoires intérieures*, his piece about Emily Brontë.

Tomorrow I'm going to the forest to gather moss, in which I'll use store carrots through the winter. The weather is still nice and warm.

29 October

Up early. Mauriac after breakfast, a couple of pages. It's slow going, but then again I have each sentence ready before going on to the next one. Sorted the Gravenstein, they're now ready for delivery. Some were rotten, some gnawed by mice, a few were unripe and thrown out. By the time I was done, I had one hundred and twenty crates packed and ready to be picked up. Maybe I can deliver one of these days.

Words Are Like Crystals – How often do we not see words turning like crystals, suddenly revealing an unexpected meaning?

If they think they can inspire interest in poetry through their dry thinking and analyses of poems, they are sorely mistaken.

22 November

One thing is good here in Ulvik: no one thinks it strange that you live as a hermit. That's how it is when the district is underpopulated.

Washed clothes, finished various tasks in the kitchen, sanded and waxed the kitchen bench-top, baked scones. And best of all, I delivered the rest of the Gravenstein apples.

Interrupted Dreams – Johan Borgen mentions that a man takes offense at and will feel out of sorts if he is not allowed to dream in peace, in other words if he is awakened too often. I'll add some thoughts to this.

I think it also most unhealthy to shock a crazy man; the very least you can do is to let him have peace. Doctors know little about the magnificent visions and dreams such people might be immersed in, and it is sad to be torn out of these. Such visions and ecstatic experiences have a particularly renewing and strengthening effect on the entire person; yes, they can be a source of bliss and hidden joy the rest of one's life, even if you should become so-called normal and healthy again.

It is terrible to be fighting demons when you know you don't have the strength; they break you down. Even those with good intentions. For they are demanding, and hardly carefree guests.

It's cold in big houses, said the man who slept outside. That's a feeling a lot of us have in this day and age. And so we choose to lie outside, where the starry heavens are great. Why is it big and cold? Because we are unable to fill it with dreams and myths. Our ancestors did, and so they did not lie outside.

There is a lot of space around writers such as Thoreau, Melville, Poe, Emerson, Whitman, Twain and Hawthorne. Great distances. There is so little that is "literary" about them; they belong to the people. I suppose they didn't pay much attention to the fashions coming out of Europe, instead they found nourishment in the great authors of the past. And all of them were closely associated with the Pioneer; they were working people themselves. They had plenty of time to read and think, they were able to get a grip on world culture from a distance, and they indicated the way forward.

8 December
Only when you understand and realize that there are those who are greater than you are, will you be able to breathe and find peace in your heart.

I have found that it is easier to endure adversity than good fortune. I have written about mat-grass elsewhere, that it will endure anything. But there is one thing it cannot tolerate: fertilizer. If it is fertilized, it will die.

10 December
Many things are on my mind these days. I think of Uncle Edmund too, perhaps especially about him. He studied at the Pacific Lutheran Academy in Tacoma, Washington. He came home when I was eighteen. It was he who taught me to immerse myself in three thinkers: Schopenhauer, Browning, and Russell. For a long time these were my gods. But it wasn't easy fitting them together; I dare say it was difficult going. I didn't have any Nietzsche on my shelf, but he lent me a copy of *Thus Spake Zarathustra.*

I never really paid attention at school, because I had so much else to read and think about. And I never did my arithmetic.

The Greatest Poets – They speak of poets these days. The greatest poets I know were those in Ward D at Valen Hospital, when I spent four years there during my first stay. Peerless men! The grandmaster was Hansen; he had a fixed route he walked in the upper garden and a fixed place at the long table. He ran everything, saw everything, knew everything. When it mattered, his voice and thoughts would reach each and every one of us. Each in our place, each in his or her role – all of us at Ward D were as if a single choir obeying its conductor. Strømme, too, was a great prophet. Espen was a great leader. With a rag tied around his right hand, he would walk in place near the toilet in the lower grounds. That giant of a man would point and give his signals. His voice was hoarse, almost inaudible; he was deaf and mute. But he was a great chief. That's why he always stood when we ate; in charge of the meal, he never sat at the table. Pål was also a chieftain, and he would suddenly stand there pointing. So was Danielsen, the old sailor, and he was always at his place by the window, giving orders, cursing and pointing. Sometimes he would sing a plaintive song. And the little Japanese guy was there, I'll never forget him.

To belong and be one of them, which I was for a time, made me proud and happy. To betray them and leave was the most despicable thing I have done. I recognized them the second time I came to Ward D, seven years later; they knew me, I thought, and I knew them. Later they didn't recognize me. They had been shocked, some operated on, and reduced to a flock of dulled, fat idiots. I caught a glimpse of Hansen; that thin man with the eagle nose had become lazy and smoked cigarettes. But sometimes I could hear him at night.

I have learned from many people. But I learned most from my father and Per Stedje. Neither of them wrote poetry, but they knew something, in their own way.

My Uncle Edmund was a hard taskmaster. He knew what great poetry was, what thinking was. For a long time, I wrote letters to him. When I was eighteen years old, he came home.

My School – First I studied with Øyvind and Ohnstad and Vikør, then I studied with Torfinn Syse, then for many years I studied with Magnus at Hagen, and I studied with Uncle Edmund, before studying with Per Stedje, then I studied at Valen Hospital. When I add what father meant to me all those years, I reckon that about covers it. You can cross out all the rest with a thick, grey line.

Hansen, Danielsen and Strømme will always be great men in my eyes.

I was never much of a he-man, I was a weakling and a coward, that's the truth of it.

"You know I need to work," I said. "Yes, but you don't have to think about what you're doing; you can choose to think what you will," said Magnus of Hagen. He claimed that's what he himself did. During the summer, he always worked as a hired hand for Nils. But I remember he would always injure himself with the axe whenever he had to trim twigs and branches – whether Shaw or Brailsford was to blame.

13 December

It's best when you can live anonymously and unnoticed. Then you're left in peace and can do what you wish, perhaps even making poems and enjoying it. To have everyone's eyes on you because you've gained a name and the newspapers are writing about you, can you think of anything more dreadful?

It's a punishment, a heavy punishment that the Lord dishes out to those who seek fame. Because all too often that's the ambition behind what a person does, be it writing or something else. It is said that you get what you ask for, and you can gain fame and renown if that is what you seek. No, Emily Dickinson was well aware of what she was doing when she would lock her poems away in a box. She had peace of mind and got something done every day. "Write them down and hide them in a book," was the advice Uncle Edmund gave me when I showed him a poem I had written when I was twenty. And I shouldn't do translation, he said, claiming it was a criminal offense. Even later I didn't do much of that.

13 May 1961

Planted potatoes, sowed peas. Been shopping. And I have looked at my poems. A collection might be taking form again. After I rewrite my poems based on all the drafts. I burned the completed collection last fall, something that I have much regretted. Now I have the poems again, I think. As soon as I have polished them up.

23 May

Sent the manuscript to the publisher. There's some excitement in this, so much effort behind such a collection of poems. And then it doesn't turn out quite the way you want.

27 May

Very depressed. It is strange how oppressed and weak I feel. No, this last stay at Valen – from the first of December 1960 to the tenth of March 1961 – was not good. I don't know how they treated me this time. I don't recall anything about electroshock, but might well have received it. Many tablets, something they call Truxal, although I have no idea what it's supposed to be good for. My sleep returned, and I'm working some, and reading a bit as well. But there is something about courage. I felt that I was on top of things, hadn't been into the hospital since 1955, and had been very strong and able-bodied. My new poetry collection was taking form, the anthology *Norske Dikt* (*Norwegian Poetry*) arrived, and I received much praise from eminent critics – in short, things were looking up for me. Had anyone told me to be careful and warned me about another bout of "madness," I would surely have dismissed it. But truth be told, I did receive warnings in dreams, and that's always been an accurate prediction. This time, however, I did not heed the warning, but the onslaught came, this time too. No, there is something or other that I can't handle, and when my sleep is disturbed and I'm not careful enough and don't take care of myself, it ends in a breakdown. Always. I have experienced that so much that I should know myself. And I do.

No, I think a person like myself pays too little heed to "the illness."

When I do a quick reckoning, these incidents have been happening every five years or so. The first time was in 1934, after my exam at Hjeltnes Agricultural School. I was home for a week or so and recovered a bit. Went to Hermansverk via Bergen. It became a long journey. From Hermansverk to Nevengården, and then I was transferred to Valen. At Christmas of 1937, I was discharged and came home.

In 1945 I was admitted to Valen again. This time I stayed there a year. In 1950 I was once again committed, with a shorter stay. In 1955 I spent half a year in the hospital. And then in 1960 I had another stay.

According to what I read, I probably suffered from schizophrenia. Catatonic schizophrenia is a diagnosis that seems to fit, but since I am doing my own analysis it may not be reliable. By and large my condition was the same, and the same thoughts grip me; I recognize them ever since that first time. I won't write more here. I will, however, say something about "the other man" in me. It's he that seizes the floor. It's a pity he is so wild.

The Other Man - In his poem "Skriket" (The Scream), Kristofer Uppdal speaks of "the other man" in us. I know well that other man, but I have not let him speak. He's an articulate lad; he doesn't have to search for words. Everything is clean and absolute, he knows as Dante knew. I understand that you must learn to trust the other. Because he'll find a way to express himself. Here is so much to do. It's really not something to fear, that other. He is wild and reckless, and he may frighten people. Time is of no concern to him, nor is distance; death does not exist for him; he has been and knows he will be, so there is no need to discuss that. In each and every way he is the opposite of the weak coward that I am, this everyday coward, this poor man. That's why you fear him, most days, when you are normal, fearful that he might seize the word, speak up, assert himself. You fear him, but deep inside you wish that he would seize the word, make himself master, because in a way you would be satisfied to be under his power. A terrible power, a reign of terror. But delicious all the same. Because he is a lad who knows how to rule. An Asiatic Khan. He is not in doubt about whom he loves. He chose one once, understands her, never doubts her, is steadfast like some eternal law. Loyal, never doubting. Know. What kind of ordinary weak fool have your habits made you? Haircut? Girlfriend? He doesn't care about such matters. He is loyal to the one he chose. You dare not grumble. No, it's a pity he is so wild. Perhaps he should be allowed to seize the word more often, in everyday situations, so he wouldn't be so wild and crazy when he does seize control.

Something is wrong here. Thinking more about him. Let him seize the floor more often, that's it.

Despair – And if despair should seize the upper hand! Even the gods had their faults. Odin lacked an eye; Thor had a deep scar in his skull from a whetstone, and he was missing a toe; Vulcan was lame; Cupid was blind; Hölderlin mad; Byron had a club-foot.

The ant never sleeps, says Emerson. That's something to think about …

13 June

I have swung the scythe many times today, but my pen has remained still.

I am wondering what to call my new collection of poems. My first suggestion was *On the Eagle's Perch* (*På Ørnetuva*) and that has stuck. But a line from one of the poems, "The dew makes the water widest," would also make a good title. It's an old saying, and I think it's rather poetic. Or I could call the collection *Dew.* Quite simply *Dew*. That might be a good solution. *On the Eagle's Perch* echoes "Skírnismál," one of the poems in the *Elder Edda*:

> On the Eagle's Perch
> shalt thou ever sit,
> back toward Manhome,
> face toward Hel.

14 July
Thinned the apple trees. Also read Emily Dickinson. Magnificent! A great actress, a loyal student of Thoreau and Emerson. No one else could write lines like:

> "To loose thee, sweeter than to gain
> All other hearts I know."

19 September
So few lives possess that wild flame, the great will that lets me understand them. Amongst those who do are Emily Brontë, Emily Dickinson, Edith Södergran, Olav Nygard, Friedrich Hölderlin and Henrik Wergeland. Most people merely accept existence as it is and try to make themselves more or less pleasing.

28 September
The literary magazine *Vinduet* (*The Window*) commemorates Rabindranath Tagore with numerous articles and translations. A well-known name to those of us who remember Eskeland's translations.

10 November
Finally! I received two copies of *On the Eagle's Perch*! It's a beautiful book; the publisher has done a fine job. If only the contents had been worthy of the cover.

12 December

I must share the news. Last night I received a call from my publisher Øyvind Dybvad at Noregs Boklag. He told me that *On the Eagle's Perch* had received The Norwegian Literary Critics Association Award for 1961! There you go! That little book held its own. He wanted me to come to Oslo on Thursday, where the award ceremony is being televised. I declined at once.

Singing Again

The river deep in my mind is singing again,
windless calm reaches me from the cool night-country,
where dream-blue peaks are mirrored
in other seas.

What are my words?
Storm-bent forests
facing north,
barren crags
facing the fire
of the coming
day.

Don't Give Me the Whole Truth

Don't give me the whole truth,
don't give me the ocean for my thirst,
don't give me heaven when I ask for light,
but give me a glint, a dewdrop, a speck,
just as the birds carry droplets of water from their bathing
or the wind a grain of salt.

Opening the Curtains

Before I go to bed, I open the curtains
– I want to see the living darkness when I wake
and the forest and the sky. I know a grave
that has no porthole to the stars.

Orion rises in the west, always on the chase,
and yet he has come no further than I have.
The cherry tree stands naked and black outside.
The hard fingernail of the morning moon
scratches the blue abyss of the sky.

Let Your Grief Go

You let go of your grief and the wind carried it away,
you threw away your pain and time washed it away.
I know you'll find stones on which to cross,
an island in the sea,
a bridge across the river Gjoll.

To a Mountain

It is as though I haven't seen you before, and yet
your stubborn claw has appeared before me every day.
Mountains are mountains – the Lord has weighed them.
I have seen their steepness and their calm,
my own arrogance in the face of the infinite;
this is a clear sign.

But early this morning I saw you: you were like an eagle
waiting for the rising sun, prepared to soar.
Now you have folded your broad wings
behind the forest tops. The dusk
and the stars are yours.

Steel Coil

Why is this coil
so tightly wound?
And you press it
flat.

This steel,
unreleased,
an anxious eagle hatchling,
a rooster that has yet to gall,
and now stretches
his neck,
more resilient
than steel.

There is no blue patience here!
This force was too great.
Shocked pride
lashed out
– and broke.

At The Seashore

She did not answer, but turned her back and walked away.
And the wind and the clouds, even the ocean turned
its darkening back; the stones of the shore slipped below,
every blade of grass, every wave moved
toward another shore.

Evening Clouds

Now the clouds roll in
with greetings from
distant shores.
It's been a long time
since they brought me tidings.
Blushing
high in the evening sky,
it's probably for
someone else.
Well, there is still
hope in this
world.

You're Searching

Just as the river on autumn nights
searches rainy dark
forests, murmuring
in fog and rain, beneath
foliage and shrubs
and sunburned spruce
– so also your memory gropes
through its own shadowy forests,
searching like that river
in the autumn night, finding again
its half-forgotten course.

The current swirls its debris
in river pools, stumbles
across stones and dawdles
with driftwood, hurries
out of clefts and
hollows, toils with
soaked stumps, juggling
sunlight and shifting shadows,
flows into the mist
and finds no land.

Farther and farther,
knowing its course,
helpless and bound;
it seems at a loss.
Staring tarns and
hungry marsh-holes
clasp it in their grasp,
it must count
each droplet from
dredged loam-banks and
washed-away sand.

Onward it chases
and even wanting to
can't stop its flight,
it butts against the cliff
to no avail, and falls
into ancient ravines;
twists like a river
in its deep canyon, wanders
through hidden valleys,
it searches and searches
in forgotten depths.

The Story of Ch'ü Yüan

This is the story of Ch'ü Yüan, the king's counselor.
Rice fields and officials bowed before him.
Until he was dismissed and became a dreamer.

Where is his kingdom now? On stars and fabled islands
far from here, where he searches for the woman he saw in a dream.
Mostly he was turned toward that other world. And as counselor
he set signs and symbols for strange roads, and he wrote
silken banners left for those who came later.

But Ch'ü Yüan complained. He could never forget
his country and the people he served – and nowhere did
the orange trees flower more intensely
than by the wells in his homeland.

I don't know why he complained. But I do know
that reality can be a harsh shore for a ship-wrecked dreamer.
And dew widens the waters.
Did he long for the bridge that hangs high in the wind?

What was he thinking when he clutched a stone and leapt
into the Mi-lo River?

The river flows, giving no answer.
That staring eye of stone is still sunk in contemplation.

Sketch

An autumn day with snowflakes flying
through the fog. A soft grey sketch
traced as in a dream.
Pines have gathered heavenly cotton
tufts in their hair,
while birches extend their slender branches
carefully, so carefully –
On frozen puddles, birds
are writing on blank pages.

To Li Po

To rule in The Heavenly Empire
must have appealed to you, Li Po.
But did you not have the whole world, the clouds and the wind,
and bliss when you were drunk?
Greater still, Li Po, is
to master your own heart.

In the River Gorge

A resounding song rings out from the gorge.
Mist drifts before the sun
shutting out the daylight.
In here, everything is dark and eerie
as in a dream.

And there she stands! It's her, on a rock in the raging river.
Is she seeking
the water spirit or
the fisherman?

The waterfall rumbles and chants, churns and chants,
sings and shoots its glittering
arc above them, strives
to enchant and ensnare
them.

Eye of the eye. A frozen moment.
Then it slips away.

He goes. Goes blindly. Further
in, into the raging sound, inside
those dark bewitching powers
– seeking himself.

Here! shouts the falls, frothing
blindly, potently
between the crags
– here anything can happen!

Rock Slide

If you're smiling, it's
far off in the distance
– in a gleam of sun
on cold snow.

All high and serious,
that's you. Who would have thought
your frozen breast-knot would burst forth
such heavy, murderous rocks?

These rocks are
dangerous and loose.
You stand there listening for them
as they fall
– hear them crashing through the woods
below you, gashing
sap-yellow tree trunks, snatching clumps of heather
and innocent creeping things, as they hurl
into the gorge.

You lift your head
into the blue, cooling your brow
in the icy stiff wind,
whistling.

Smoke

Light and cheerful the smoke rises
from the chimney in the woods
where the young couple lives.

Joyfully they offer
stout birch and fat pine
to the powers of light.

Above the miser's farm
the smoke is sparse and thin.
Hard times –
little is given
to God.

You won't see
your own smoke.
Often I sat
dark
as Cain.

An Old-Fashioned Norwegian

I always greet nard-grass like an old acquaintance,
not because he's particularly friendly; I recall he'd poke me
sharply through my woolen shirt when we carried in the dried hay,
but for a novice with the scythe
he was a good taskmaster.
Now you only see him in the outfields.

Nardus stricta is his Latin name.
I knew him long before I learned
that fancy name; he's an ill-tempered lad
who resists the scythe,
white-headed and with
yellow fire-ants amongst his roots,
flint-blue and bristly
– your only chance to take him is
in the early morning, when
he's still lop-eared
with dew.

Kinck wrote of an old-fashioned Norwegian.
Nard-grass is of that kin,
thriving in drought, thriving in sun
and in scrawny soil
– but feed him fertilizer
and he'll die.

The Meadow at Kvannskorane

The Hakastad kin never rested as well
as when that last hay bundle, wrapped in a red
petticoat, had been sent speeding down the wire
from Kvannskorane meadow.
When they sat down at last, high up
on that sunny slope, the cool breeze
felt good and well-earned.

No one makes hay now at Kvannskorane, though the grass
glows just as green above the valley. You have to tilt
your head way back to see that meadow.
When I was a boy, the transport wire had
already been taken down. The Kvannskorane Wire
– we voiced the name with awe, our eyes following its path
back up the mountainside, back into history and legend.
We thought it a pity the wire was gone.

The Message Stick

Surely it would come.
You knew
it had to come.
Now it is here.

You tremble
– joy sings in you.
Your loneliness had
raised walls higher
than heaven.

So often you think of
that message stick.
Those golden
wings.

The Chopping Block

It's tough to be
the block beneath the axe
– I've felt it.
But when they
chose me, I learned:
just hold still and
stay silent.

Up the slope lumbermen
start floating logs.
Let them chop away
here in the yard!
I swagger and strut
with my splintery head.

The Sawbuck

Strong-bodied, straddling,
he lifts his fresh-hèwn horns,
awaiting logs and saw,
logs and saw.

He who was once
a swaying storm, a brightly
living dream.

Sawdust piles up around him
in rotting heaps, while
saw-teeth rasp his back and he becomes
gashed, skew-legged and grey.
Winter and summer he stands
in the yard, his only company
the chopping block.

God knows what
the night tells him,
God knows
what he's pondering
out under the stars.

Autumn Has Come from the Summerlands

Autumn has come from the summerlands,
bringing heavy gifts:
here is ripe fruit,
here is wine!

He lingers a while on the grassy slopes,
scattering torn paper in the wind.

High are the heavens,
deep is hell
– the mind churns,
the mirror trembles.

One morning I see his white hair
in the distant mountains.

An Evening In November

The weather is clearing now. This night brings frost.
I inspect the orchard knowing apples
still hang in those high branches. I'm still hoping
for mild weather, firewood in the shed,

cabbage gathered and piled, new trees
planted. There should still be time to prepare
that new orchard. But I see autumn recede,
the loam is freezing and snow is creeping

halfway down the hillside – I know there isn't time.
But I'll bring those apples in, I'll find a way
and have at least that one less worry.

To the west hangs the new moon large and sharp
as the autumn air, eager for its harvest.
I won't miss the dark sun-bound earth.

It's Cold in Big Houses

It's cold in big houses.
I notice this in the autumn
when the first snowflakes are falling
and frost hardens the fields.
Then my loneliness is huge and barren,
cracked open under my roof,
and the axe-blows echo in the frozen woods.
My forest is the forest
in her forest.
My mountain is the mountain
in her mountain
– and the day is but a crack of light
in her night.
The few people and creatures that I meet,
who are out at dawn puttering about
with pine needles and twigs,
leaving footprints through frosted grass,
are shadowy ghosts in her dream.

Winter Day

What does this strange light want with us?
This is a day under white stars,
dreams are sprouting under the moon.

The mountain has words deep within,
but its breast is stiff, its beard frozen.
The river-mouth answers with a brief glint, briefly open,
and the pines offer up their resin drops.
The goldcrest shakes down snow,
the frosty muzzle of the horse quivers.
Firewood twists out cold fat,
and the frost eats up the axe-blow.

But now the pinnacle butts the sun-disc, splinters it
into a thousand shards, squinting towards distant spheres.
The spruce-candles on the ridge are snuffed out,
and trees settle into their groves for the night.
The river sighs in its gorge, its longing for the sea chilled
to ice, and the stones sleep beneath the snow,
holding green dreams in their hearts.

Beneath the Stars

What drives me out
beneath this hard morning sky?
These demanding blue stars,
what do they want?

These mountains promise nothing
– they yield only to let the rivers run
and the fjords fill up. They feel
nothing beneath the snow.

But these wooded slopes
bare their need beneath the stars.
It's my wound, my grief
black as iron, that lies bleeding
and vows to turn green and sing again.

Kuppern on Skates in Squaw Valley

I also won a prize on skates, coming in
fourth in a school race when I was eight,
after Leiv, who won.
But they had skates with steel blades
and I had only iron.
I bought mine from the watchmaker,
choosing the ones with
the biggest curlicues.

And now in Squaw Valley,
Kuppern is on his way to victory!
I never planned on racing the ten-thousand meter,
but our words take on a wilder tone
and my mother has a fierce grip
on her walking stick.

You Know a Spring?

Do you know a spring in the frozen woods,
do you know the heart,
lonesome, that rises?
A place to rest and quench your thirst,
reflect on your troubles and tend
your rumpled feathers?

Spruce Forest

Hungering, he reaches from dark valleys toward the heights,
behind him – all the grief of this earth.
Kindle our tops, quicken our light!
The heavens open an eye,
turns toward another firmament.
The perplexed forest fumbles in its darkness.
A few frozen stars hang in the scrawny tree-tops.

Winter Still Lives in This Light

Winter still lives in this light
and sleeps in the first grass,
which is ice-green and cold
when he leaves.
The cherry trees bloom as though
they're lifting snow, laying sisterly
cheeks on the glaciers above.
Dandelions cut through last year's straw
kindling frost-yellow fires.

The Blue Land

Here I am safe – here are oaks by the drystone walls,
here the fjord gleams between sea-worn mountains.
From where I stand behind my window
those huge oaks
have the deep hues
of an old oil painting,
on that enamel-blue sky
forgotten clouds
hurry away from the sea.

Oak leaves in autumn sun!
This blue land, land of mountains, land of sea
and ages behind me glow
with colors that have
true weight.

Today is cool and there are snowflakes in the air,
naked branches reach like claws
seeking warmth and the last ozone.
I walk this blue land
beneath falling rock.
One day Yggdrasil will be bare.

The Wave

That wave chasing the star
rages once again, shatters, hesitates,
combs through stubborn sea-wrack and debris
yields darkly, and with an angry eye gleaming green,
pulls the evening glow into its deep grave.

Snowy Evening

Give away your darkness and be rich.
Like some evening after snow.
The fields are rich and the uplands too,
snow sprinkles from the pine branches,
and the houses are rich – safe
for life and hearth.

The sleeping earth knows
its own splendor.
Heaven's frosty brow
is full of stars.

Clear as an Autumn Sky

Your spirit's eye can be
clear as an autumn sky
and so tranquil,
but also dim
as misted glass
and blind
as a frozen pane.

At dawn one day you sat
in the feathers of the sun-eagle
– do you recall?

But you wavered
in death's
forest, and you did not see
that a seal was placed
upon the stars.

Yet you are witless,
believing the day
can light your way
through
this world. When Oedipus
glimpsed
a dark fate
once hidden,
he no longer needed
daylight.
What use
is your inner eye
unless *one*
makes you a seer?

Give thanks to your God
when light and lightning strike,
shattering
your blind
pride, opening
your very core!
It is not the stone
that is blind.

Clear as an autumn day…
This fragile sound
as though from ice
– is something
shattered? Wells
may dwindle, they know
their source.

Wasn't It You?

Wasn't it you who came dancing in the sunlight
between willows and hazel groves
– your laughter that rose in a dazzling song,
clucking deeply, so deeply,
and wasn't your hair swinging freely?
Yes, it was you.

And wasn't it you who stood on the hillside
sticking needles into the sunny wind
so tears filled my eyes?
Yes, it was you.

Song, Tread Lightly On My Heart

Song, tread lightly on my heart,
as lightly as heather blooming above a moist bog,
a bird perched on a lake after a single night of frost.
Were you to break that crust of my grief
your song would drown.

This Is Not the Kingdom of the Poor

This is not the kingdom of the poor
nor a house of grief,
but take your hat off
when you enter.
You cannot know
where love burns bright
and the good spirit
keeps watch.
No one reads here.
No one writes here.
But God will find
both the sleeping
and the waking
heart.

To a Painting by Nikolai Astrup

Is it possible they dreamed this: to meet
on this Earth, in this place where bird-cherries
and apple trees stand amidst the wood sorrel,
blossoming by the fjord on such a lush-green

spring eve? To be together, plant berries, sow
row after row of herbs in hallowed soil
behind dry-stone walls raised around sacred
groves by those who wandered here before us?

In their kingdom they are sowing their field.
The spring eve is lit by dreams and new growth.
Still unaware of the luminous one

in the snowdrifts – walking across the waters.
But when night comes, they see the moon out there
robed in gold, a gentle miracle.

The Wheat Field

An old woodcut of Tower Bridge
and a color lithograph of a wheat field.
There are no other pictures in Ward D.

Tower Bridge rises sooty above the river.
But my eyes are fixed on that wheat field.
A golden sea of wheat.

It is nothing like other fields.
Have all these dreamer-eyes moved it
into a heaven of its own?

A mild autumn blue heaven
without reapers or scythes.

Droplets On the Eastern Wind
Dropar i austavind
1966

Overleaf: In the fruit-growing district of Hardanger, most of the rain comes from the North Sea to the west. When rain arrives on an easterly wind in the summer, it is usually most welcome. The title may also refer to literary and spiritual impulses that Hauge for decades had been gleaning from the Far East!

Hauge with his orchard ladder. Photo: Odd Nerbø. (Archives of the Olav H. Hauge Centre, Ulvik, Norway.)

Excerpts from Hauge's Journals – through autumn 1966

16 June 1962

Let your outer work be the symbol of your inner work.

Chinese Poetry – I just received *The Penguin Book of Chinese Verse.* A truly wonderful and enriching book! An excellent introduction, with commentary and brief biographies.

20 June

Up early. Read some Chinese Verse, and am constantly discovering wonderful things.

Went shopping. Made dinner. Now I'm going to cut grass.

Aage Marcus: *Den Blå Drage* (*The Blue Dragon*) is a book about China and Chinese culture. The author focuses especially on Taoism and Buddhist mysticism, while also taking time to dwell on Chinese art and literature. It's a good, accessible book. I have read that the Chinese say "thread" or "warp" where we say "classical." That's a much better word. A thread stretches into the past, as well as into the future, and it requires our "weft" – our action here and now. Some of the sages we encounter belong to that thread.

Marcus writes well about Zen. This form of Buddhism is often studied in the West today, especially after the war. Also fascinating is his chapter on calligraphy, which the Chinese hold in higher esteem than painting. This is a book well worth owning and reading.

In the chapter on Zen, Aage Marcus writes: "What makes Zen particularly important culturally, is that *satori* is not viewed as the final goal, but rather a gateway."

8 August

Rain. Grey. Foggy. Every tree and bush was full of thrushes when I came out this morning. Drizzle and thrush. Had to bring in the raspberries today, but didn't finish. No, we need more sunny weather in the days ahead.

Payment for Poems, 100 Kroner from *Magasinet for alle* (the magazine for everyone). "You're Searching" will appear in number thirty-four, in the last week of August. That's great! And the best thing is that the editors requested the poem. When you receive money for a poem, you should use the money for something that pleases your muse, says Robert Graves – "Buy plain editions of the better poets or plant a mulberry tree." Yes, Graves knew how to put it.

Recollections – During those years that I lived a truly spiritual life, they called me sick and locked me up. For four whole years. I recall that I sometimes decided to remain watchful at night to see what was happening. And I witnessed amazing things! The night was full of voices and signals. There was a great ongoing conversation in the realm of spirits. Not just of earthlings, but also from other realms. The living and the dead, there seemed to be no distinction. I often reflected on how foolish I had been, not to learn to listen to these amazing things earlier. Instead, I slept and I believed others did the same. No, now at last I understand how little I know about people; some – and far more than you know – might well have been paying attention, ever since they were children, and perhaps now were great in the realm of spirits – maybe they were familiar with it, partaking in that conversation, voicing opinions that were listened to by those who really run things. It became clear to me that training was required. I understood that the written word was foolish nonsense, for sleepyheads like myself who didn't really know what was going on in the world and who didn't really understand the spiritual life. And poets, even Henrik Wergeland and Robert Browning, were mere shadows. Pale shadows. For now I heard and saw much that was far more beautiful than all the things they chattered about. Oh poets, for I thought of them often those years, were mere shadows, simple-minded fools who slept and messed about and busied themselves with writing, sleeping at night and otherwise walking through this world blind and deaf. A poor woman, even an illiterate one, can go so much further and stand much higher amongst the spiritual giants than any poet, if she only learns to listen and interpret the signals and voices that echo through the heavens at night and, yes, even during the day.

I shall write no more of this. I have fallen back to the vices of my youth. During the night I sleep, no longer listening for the spirits, but instead I search for wisdom in books as before. Books! It often occurs to me how much my father held them in contempt. But it is strange to reflect on how much he nevertheless knew, even though he had never read a book.

Strength and Self-Discipline. The Advent of the Spiritual – We should not allow ourselves to become confused, for much of what we call madness is confusion. When for the first time I found myself in the midst of a powerful spiritual storm, I was twenty-five years old and in poor physical shape; furthermore I lacked self-discipline and let myself be confused, although I won't deny a certain "mental derangement."

It has happened again on several occasions, and it is at least partly due to confusion and a lack of insight about the unveiling of the spiritual, which can be a terrifying thing.

Many people have experienced such storms – that's easy to see based on their writings. One way to deal with it is to dampen the storm with drugs, although that is not without its dangers. That's just like throwing water or sand or soil onto a fire; it might smoulder unseen and suddenly break out in an unexpected place.

For spirit appears as storm and lightning and may act like a storm in our life, that should be clear enough to everyone. Others may experience it as a gentle breeze or blessed good weather.

Hence knowledge about the ways and unveilings of the spirit are vital. I realized that too late. I was, as Shakespeare puts it: "too lightly timbered for so loud a wind."

At such times, i.e., when you are spiritually aware, you may feel like an electric battery that emits a flow of blue sparks towards the stars. Finally you become like a pole in a force field, lying there stiff and sparkling, as the current flows through you.

I see that the psychoanalyst Ola Raknes, a student of Wilhelm Reich, writes about Cosmic Energy. There are fields of such energy extending through space, straight as the threads of a tapestry, and very unyielding. I don't need to say anything more about this.

Our earth and the planets are but specks.

Trances and such are merely lower states of consciousness experienced on the path to cosmic awareness, which is conscious and willed, not indulgent.

To cling to reality and ordinary things, that cannot be engaged in too often. At least not for me. It's important to grip the earth firmly, so the storm does not carry you away. That is my experience. The voices and visions – they mean you no harm.

5 December

A Word on Baudelaire – "Any healthy man can live three days without food, but without poetry never, and those who claim the contrary are out of their minds."

23 March 1963

Rough night. Slept little. I have been well for a long time. Now I lay there feeling giddy and fantasising. A lot of nonsense! Looks like snow is coming. Perhaps the change in weather made me restless. I don't know. No, it was just me. But! I'm on my feet now – coffee, breakfast, a fire in the stove, and ready for Baudelaire!

24 August

Wherever I look, the woods are lit up by the rowanberries. The days are quiet, mostly grey and cloudy. Let there be some sunny weather soon!

7 October

Delivered the last apples. Altogether I have delivered eight hundred and fifty crates; I've never had more apples. Today I'm harvesting potatoes. It was hard work, but I managed.

14 September 1964

Higher consciousness has its own memory, which comes to the fore, clearly and vividly, when you are in that state (cosmic consciousness). The ordinary man, we might well call him the workman in the garden, has no recollection or only a faint memory of states of higher consciousness. Thus, such memories of earlier or distant experiences can only be remembered when they reclaim sovereignty of your inner life. When they do, the memories of those past moments glow vividly before you. Ecstasy must come to you, if past ecstatic states are to be remembered and be fully felt. Actually I would not use the word *memory*, because they do not act as memories as such, but rather as currents of fire coursing through the whole of your being. You become like a coil in a force field, lying down and stretched out, trembling in the presence of mighty forces. Should you try to stand up or walk, you will feel like a branch in a storm, or a burning tree. Those force currents sometimes flow from certain directions, they are powerful and relentless. The voices that accompany this sound like they're coming from other realms: the currents, the fire, also seem to come from a distant space. But – and here I would like to recount one of my own experiences – the forces, the fiery currents that come from various directions, from all directions, can be so strong that you spin like a spool, knowing neither inside nor outside, and, sensing this chaos of fiery rays, of powerful currents, you become wholly confused. I myself have experienced this. The shiver, the sigh or storm that follows in the wake of all this, can be immensely strong; it might feel like you're about to swept away, like a leaf on the wind; the room is bathed in a bluish light, or if you're outside the field, the sea, the mountains and sky take on a new tinge. Often you have to seize something solid so as not to be swept away, grasp hold of a tangle of grass, claw your fingers into the sand – that's how it often feels. Worst is the trembling and current felt under the open sky. I felt safer indoors.

I rarely touch on such matters in my poetry. "The Wheat Field" speaks of calmer moments, whereas one other touches on the more bursting experience. Only partly is my own experience portrayed. Diamond sleep and moments of illumination (such as journeys to distant stars) are hinted at in "Luminous Spaces" (Rømder av glans). I think I made the right decision not to publish the vast material I have from the years I was gone, altogether well over six years. Many times I have ridden out the storm without ending up in the madhouse, even in my youth. When catastrophe struck – in other words I ended up in the hospital – I believe the primary cause is that I forgot to eat, and in addition fell into a feverish delirium. Or quite simply, and I suppose that's the truth of the matter, that my visions and the intensity of my experiences were so overwhelming that I followed every impulse blindly, that I believed in the voices, and thus acted so strangely that people must have been convinced I had lost my mind. And I suppose that's right, when people lack control. I have been immersed in my own tasks, such as sitting in my underwear at home directing an orchestra; what are ordinary people to think of such behavior?

Ecstatic states of terrifying intensity can often be of a nature where others think you have lost your mind. And afterwards there are often periods of powerlessness, confusion and lack of awareness; I cannot say for sure, but I believe that is the case. I do know one thing, that I was lucky to spend four years at Nevengården and Valen without being "cured," since electroshock and all these medicines that they use now had not yet been introduced. I was allowed to write and dream, see visions, experience ecstasy day after day, year after year, without anyone doing anything to me. Whether I was shut away or restrained – which I often was – didn't matter. The ecstasy, dreams, visions and voices reached me all the same. I never thought it a problem to be restrained or shut away in a solitary cell, and really don't have any complaints.

The electroshock treatment came later, that's true.

My last stay at Valen was more enriching, because I did not receive shocks. I suppose the tablets they use calm you down, but they did not darken my inner life. On the other hand, I must enter a proviso, because I am unsure whether they gave me the tablets that dim your mind and kill your imagination. That's all I have to say on the matter. You have to get your grounding back, if you're going to live in this world.

Except during periods when I felt helpless, I have not experienced any suffering or felt particularly depressed during the years I was gone. I have seen much that is ugly and terrible, I have witnessed that side of life, too. But I think I was born with a happy disposition, and I always have been happy, even though I've sometimes hung my head.

10 November

"No man ought to make the fence more important than the thing fenced in," says the *Talmud*. I have nothing to add to these wise words, which are applicable to many things.

Pănini- Pănini wrote a Sanskrit grammar well before 300 BCE. Linguists say it is the best book on grammar ever written.

Arabic has more than five-hundred words for camel.

Some Bantu languages have twenty genders.

3 July 1965

Only when your broken hopes turn to grief does the bridge open – the bridge that carries you over everyday life.

A calm, cold, clear evening. I hear a river singing, perhaps several rivers. The hillsides are green, dotted with patches of snow that resemble grazing sheep. Yes, I say tonight I'm holding my head high again, perhaps for the first time in years. In recent years I've been burdened, depressed, without hope of rising again. And this last year I've suffered fevers and tumultuous thoughts – about *her*. I know it's madness. All the same; I now realize that I must, I must, I must tread on my hopes again, I must. The worst of it is that my studies have deteriorated, and thus I have deteriorated as well. You enter new rooms that really only belong in your wildest dreams – and behave like an ordinary man! Because the dream *could* become reality before you know it. It can! But you are too bound to your frailties. My God, how foolish a man can be!

14 July

Saw the doctor. Folkedal says there's nothing wrong with my heart; it's in fine shape, he says. *Your chest pains must be due to some sort of myalgia, muscle pains. There is no point in sending you to a specialist or the hospital for further examination, because they won't find anything.* He's done that once before. Angina pectoris is something else entirely, he says. Yes, I suppose I should be grateful for such words. *But you do have arrhythmia,* he says.

There are times when I have been so alive that every tiny thing speaks to me.

I know that when the trembling starts, and I forget to eat and sleep, disaster soon strikes. All the times I have been "ill," as it's called, I have been enchanted by the visions and voices. I haven't resisted, and have left this world. Coolly now! Coolly now!

Buckets of cold water help. And hard work, hard work!

Unfortunately! I have my clear moments, then I fall back into sloth.

2 September

In the beginning, my poems resembled the gardens we learned to draw in gardening school. Straight paths, straight flowerbeds, square lawns, well-pruned trees and bushes. Slate and gravel. Now, however, I let nature and function form my garden. I keep the paths I walk open. Clover and plantain grow in the yard, wildflowers and grass grow by the walls. A large patch of white yarrow has found a place by the steps; now they're flowering beautifully. That's how poems should be.

22 September

Picked the rest of the Gravensteins from the trees in the flat part of the orchard, only a few on the hillside left. I have many thoughts today, ideas for good poems. Didn't have time to complete them. I'm tired now. "By China's Door" is good.

I spoke of memories. They mean you no harm. Trust that!

But beware of the world! They don't understand you, and many ill things are said of you. Let it be! Loneliness, surely you know what that is!

I am writing poetry again. I'm fine for a fortnight or so, but often I forget to eat enough and sleep far too little. Then soon I am lying there in feverish dreams, exalted and kind of in a trance. Visions and wild thoughts, until finally I start believing in my own delusions. These tend to be of the same kind. I hear voices and those play a key role. Often they are benevolent, and I reflect on that. The real world doesn't exist any more. My world is mythical and magical; that may not be the right word, but poetic is too weak, that's not quite apt; it's surely irrational, but still very orderly, although everything is obeying supernatural laws.

I'm sure it's possible for me to conjure forth all these memories again, but doing so is frightening and dangerous. *Trance* is too weak a word, as is *ecstasy*, to describe these states of mind.

A calculated poem is rarely good, only one that is seen! It's not a question of distance. It can be seen and experienced even though the event happened far away or long ago, even five thousand years ago.

My point is that calculated poems rarely are any good. What you write about must be seen by your spirit, and the words must come flying to you as birds, or have been in the forge until they glow. Otherwise they'll be dry and merely seem cold-forged.

Don't forget cold water. Drink water! When the trembling starts, drink water! When heaven and hell are loose, and I am compelled to only work, until I finally sleep from exhaustion.

Truth

Truth is a shy bird,
a Roc flying
outside time
– sometimes before,
sometimes after.
Some say she
doesn't exist,
those who have seen her
stay silent.
I have never thought of truth
as a tame bird,
but if she were
you should stroke her feathers
and not frighten her up into some corner
lest she turn her owlish eyes and claws against you.
Others say truth is
a cold knife-edge.
She is both
yin and *yang*,
the snake in the grass,
and the goldcrest who escapes the eagle
when the eagle thinks he's highest.
I have also seen
truth dead:
eyes like a frozen hare.

One Word

One word
– one stone
in a cold river.
One more stone –
I need many stones
to make it across.

Mountain Wind

You were a fierce cold mountain gale.
Until a dark windbreak rose up and
splintered your power. Death.
Now you sneak about – a humbled breeze
along lukewarm mountains.

Wobbly Boulder

What a remarkable place
to settle on, this barren
ledge, poised
on the precipice.
Don't you value your victory?

Stone Age Grave

The ant stumbles
through the world.
As does man.
A wretched creature.

But you
left
your bones
as witness
that you were here,
white bones
and a clay jar
in a small
hollow.

You were brave
and carried life.
A dream flickered in your heart.
A strong fire.

There Is Nothing Scary

There is nothing scary
about the grasshopper whetting his scythe.
But when the woodlouse is whispering,
you'd better beware.

Kvasir the Wise

Beware, Kvasir the Wise,
do not enter my cave
lest I strike you dead,
and drain your blood
for brewing mead!

I have no need of that broth,
for in my mountain I have
the very source – though
surely that godly brew
will lend strength
and fervor!

The Owl

Trees in the garden
glow with ripe berries,
the thrush flurries in.
And there sits the owl
– its round head staring.
The thrush turns,
and startled flies off.
Even though the owl
perched in the sun
is dead, its tree
– black as night –
is terrifying.

Adrift

My life is adrift on the Arctic Ocean.
Sheathed in ice, my ship sits in desolate waters.
I listen to each creaking and cracking;
has that current I trusted fallen still?
The wind sweeps across ice-fields, but on the heavens
old constellations still shine brightly.
Strong is my desire to complete the passage.
My dreams suckle on heavy star clusters.

We're not Sailing the Same Sea

We're not sailing the same sea,
though it may appear so.
Rough-hewn timber and iron on deck,
sand and cement in the hold.
Low in the water, I plow
through heavy seas,
wailing in the mist.
You sail your paper boat,
your dream filling its blue sail
– so soft that wind, so gentle the wave.

Leiv Eiriksson

Black ship on grey seas.
Days and nights under sail.
Uncertain is the power of Ægir;
perhaps this sea has no end?
Still you sail westward
trusting that the sea will find a shore.

Sveigdir

Many went before you, Sveigdir,
and many went after;
yet no man knows where you wandered.
When we met, you lay badly wounded;
we broke bread, parted.
You had been an outlaw and
a merman – the soles of your feet
still glittering with fish-scales.
Will you emerge again from that mountain?

Ogmund Rides Home

You deserved to ride home.
No Crusader ever journeyed further.
On the White Sea you were blocked by ice,
and you sailed so far along the rivers of Russia!
You stood before Jericho with an ash spear
carried all the way from Sponheim.

Now you ride for home across the Hungarian plains.
The evening sun glows
and a northerly wind greets you.
When at last you see the snowy hood of Mount Vassfjøro,
that's when tears flow inside your helmet.

In Memory of Old Vamråk

Every morning he stood up in his cell and sang.
They could have shut him up in an empty barrel,
he still would have praised God through the cork-hole.

Ophelia

You are no enigma, Ophelia,
you're only the riddle a life and heart are.
How impossibly tangled life can be!
Where would we go
if we didn't have grief and death?
Dance, Ophelia. Sing!
Scatter rose petals around you,
flee into a darker room,
it's more pleasant there, and your days
are not so hard.
Pierced by the burning arrows of anguish,
sing, Ophelia! Dance!
The moat is scattered with rose petals.

I Stand Here, You See

I stand here, you see.
I stood here last year too, you see.
I'll keep standing here, you see.
I'll take it, you see.
You know nothing, you see.
You just got here, you see.
How long shall we stand here?
We have to eat, you see.
I stand when I eat too, you see.
And throw my bowl against the wall.
We have to rest, you see.
We have to sleep, you see.
We have to piss and shit too, you see.
How long shall we stand here?
I stand here, you see.
I'll take it, you see.
I'm going to stand here, you see.

Up On Top

After wandering far on impossible trails
you're up on top.
Hardships couldn't stop you,
you trod them under, climbed higher.

That's how *you* see it. After life had
tossed you aside, and you ended up on top
like a one-legged wooden horse on the rubbish heap.
Life is merciful, it blinds you and offers illusions,
and fate shoulders your burden:
folly and pride become crags and bogs,
hate and anger become wounds from the enemy's arrows,
and the doubt that gnawed at you becomes
a cold, dry gorge.

You step through the door.
On your hearthstone the cauldron lies toppled,
hostile black feet splayed in the air.

Guard Stones

Now and then the road
crosses a plain.
There it won't kill you
should you fail to follow it,
but people do.
Most often you've got
a rockface on one side
and the abyss on the other,
so you better keep to the road.
The rockface blocks you,
while the guard stones leer
like a row of teeth:
Keep to the road!
Jagged guard stones,
cut from the crag
by staunch quarrymen,
turn their sharp edge
toward you:
we'll split your skull.
Keep to the road!

Schoolyard

When the bell rings
for the first lesson,
the schoolyard abandoned
– a concrete poem.

Footprints in crowded
groups near the entrance,
where they discussed
moon rockets and the victor's
times at St. Moritz.

Half-finished snowmen
have been left
by the youngest.

Along the walls are
the places of the loners;
one for him and one for her.

On the outhouse wall
are splattered snowballs,
in the restroom a broken window,
above the principal's door
a contemptuous splotch.

Letters writ in snow:
Solveig + Knut
Åse + _ _   He managed
to erase his name.

Out on the yard
a hollow from a fight,
drops of nose-blood
and a green mitten.

The Hay Wire

I learned that you should wind up
the hay wire onto a spool.
But Anders insisted
that we just use a stick.
Many of the lads liked Anders.
It's all right to be taking down long hay wires.
You can let your mind wander and sing and think of pretty girls.

The Estuary

As long as she was open,
there was hope.
But her flow dwindled and she grew cold,
until finally she froze over, and the wind covered her with snow.
Now they've drilled deep into the heart
of the mountain lake, tapping icy depths,
and the whole bay is open!

The Wall

Old stones
make a good wall
if you lay them well,
fit them tight.
Perhaps these were badly cut,
uneven, they still have patches
of lime or old cement
– you can see they've been
in a wall before.
Best to quarry new stones,
cut them as you please,
that way you'll get good lines
and a clean face.
Then you'll have a stout wall
you can call your own.

Poetry Today

Poetry today is cheap
– cheap to write,
cheap to buy,
like toy cars
and plastic planes for kids.
Verses don't strain
your thoughts much either.
They manage well without pretty feathers,
but if they have them,
so much the better.
Young people think of words
as building blocks
and can manage
the most incredible things;
but can they,
with a mental roll of the dice,
change human nature?
To portion out wisdom
from the Bible or Talmud
is well and good,
and anything may be of use,
even your own life.
There is still
a gnarled birch,
and your neighbor will quote
a saying from his father.

The Germans make poems
most efficiently and cheaply,
and the Japanese aren't
at a loss either
– even their emperor
is said to have written
more than a thousand poems.
But I don't suppose those are
for sale.
Mao Tse-tung sets his poems
to march: work songs,
battle hymns, threatening
admonitions,
and fashions words
into truths.

Winter Has Forgotten

Winter has forgotten its white cows on the mountain,
now they graze on the green slopes up there.
But the grass and spring sun are too strong,
that snowy herd grows scrawnier by the day.

They Didn't Think

They didn't think.
They moved blindly.
Sometimes they stood
looking
– thinking.
That must be something new.

The Skating Race

You start out even with the favorite.
You know you cannot match his pace,
yet you burst forward
and summon all your strength,
for a while you match his stride.

Then he glides away from you,
glides away from you, glides away
– soon he leads by a full lap.

At first you feel shame;
then a strange calm comes over you.
Why not let the favorite race ahead!

And thus you find your own rhythm,
racing against yourself.
None of us can do more.

Let Me Be Like the Dung Beetle

Grief settles over me
and pushes me down into the warm grass.
Let me still move,
test my strength, lift the sod
– let me be like that dung beetle on a spring day,
when he digs his way out from the dung heap.

A Seed

A seed of righteousness
took root in my heart, grew
and became a salty fire.
I fed it, offering
fatty sacrifice.
And that fire became a dragon!

Winter Morning

When I woke this morning the windows were frozen shut
but I still glowed from a good dream.
And the stove poured out its warmth
from a log it had enjoyed all night long.

Rivers Meet

Rivers meet, each from its own mountain.
Grasping each other by the hand
they blend their song, their blood.

They carry on, of one mind and stronger,
far less likely to stumble on the stones.
No one shall wade dry-shod now!

And I Was Grief

And I was grief and dwelled in a cave.
And I was pride and built beyond the stars.
Now I build in the nearest tree,
and each morning when I wake
the pine threads its needles with gold.

Autumn Fishing

The river carries
shards of ice,
it's thin,
bites hard,
rages between the stones.
Cropped ash-trees
line the riverbank, gray,
each shoot and black bud
starkly visible,
the alder thicket is ragged,
rimed, drowsy.
The trout wriggle
cold and firm.

Spring in the Mountains

Today the snowdrifts
dance like stags in the sunlight.
The river hurries homeward
carrying winter away.
The golden plover has arrived
and these grassy green slopes.

Spring by the Fjord

A blue haze curls up
from the plowed fields,
the shore is green
this year too.
My sorrows have been sent
to shadier pastures,
a black snow that
smothers the heather.

The Wind Has Much to Tell This Spring

The wind has
    so much
        to tell

this spring. It's years
    since I
        heard him;

he huffs
    and puffs
        in barren trees

wills them to waken,
    break into green!
        Then he shakes

the ridge-beam,
    wills us to waken!
        Then he's back

in the trees,
    grabs them
        shakes them,

sharply
    with rough gusts!
        Sneaks

around corners,
  pilfers from the pile
    of last year's leaves

flicks up
  a swirl
    of them –

they're dry now
  dry –

scampers across
  the field, whirls up
    dust

returns, tries on
  an old black hat
    and is gone –

Come back!
  Come back!

Willow

The willow
stands as yellow
as last year,
though fewer see her.
Nor do we hear
flutes now.

Mountain Farm

Here the river churns.
Here the wind sighs.
Here wolfsbane blooms again.

An old horse has gnawed
the knoll barren.
Amidst buzzing flies
near the horse apples
tufts of long grass grow.
He won't touch those.

Goats lie resting
on rocks and boulders
chewing their cud,
ignoring us as best they can.
They will climb any mountain
to nibble the peaks.

Rockface Behind the Falls

We're awe-struck and terrified
by your companions as well,
those who tremble
dripping cold water.
We don't see your face
although we know you're there:
a strong spine,
your obstinacy unbroken
beneath this wild beast
that throws itself
over you, frothing
at the mouth,
wrestling
in green rage.

Late one summer
the wind might brush
silken rags aside.
Then at last
we'll see your
features – not
some cool green,
worn-down
expression,
but a white-
scrubbed
innocence.

The Skerry

Many skerries in the sea.
But it is this
skerry
that saves your life.

The Islet

Solitary, exiled
far from land,
the islet struggles
in his rough mountain lake.
On calm nights,
when the waters sleep,
he feels the bedrock below,
spreads out heavy and huge
and becomes one with the land.

Floating Log

Shoot
the rapids,
– I'm through!
Now I want to rest, said the log,
circling slowly on the eddy.

Seed

No place to grow here.
Don't put down roots,
don't unfold flowers!
Stay hard and whole
to save your life!

Crossing the Quagmire

These are the roots of all the trees that died,
that's why you can walk
dry-shod across the quagmire.
Roots like these stay firm a long time,
they may have lain here for centuries.
Under the moss, there is still
some dark remnant of them.
They are still here and
carry you safely across.

When you push out onto the mountain lake,
you suddenly sense the memory – the cold corpse
of the man who drowned himself, he helps
hold up your frail boat.
He, the insane one, trusted his life
to water and eternity.

Whirl

It's only
a whirl.
You shouldn't
indulge in a whirl,
they say.
You too
would whirl
had you only
followed them.
But you kept
to the straight
and narrow path.
Who's to say
what's right:
a whirl or
will of steel.
I suppose
one's right
this time,
the other
another time.
That's true
when you run
and when
you sing.

Windmills

Those sails, made for catching wind,
don't need a big gust before they
turn and the windshaft spins.
But in a storm I would lash them
or take them down.
Naked stumps will have
struggle enough.

Should

I should
unwrap
loosen up
brighten up
and strut forth,
do as the juniper,
defy rain and hail!

Prod

We need a prod
now and then.
Or we stop, seize up.
There might be a speck
of dust in your watch – that
needs to be swept away
before it ticks again.
Some of us need niggling
till stubble grows
on our old chin.

You Were the Wind

I am a boat
without wind.
You were the wind.
Was that the course I meant to sail?
Who cares to chart a course
with a wind like that!

The Dipper

You brave dipper!
Daringly you dive
deeply into cold black streams
after the food you need,
shake water from your feathers
sing a cheerful song,
and dive again.
Ice bites at your feet.
Snow-rimed heavy winter
fires your heart.
There is still an opening
to flowing water.

Rising River

Fish don't fuss
should the river rise.
But that poor beaver frets
about his lodges.

Saw

Rrrip,
says the saw.
Fine firewood.
She speaks
her mind, that saw.

Sledgehammer

I am just
a sledgehammer.
I lean here.
I only make the effort
when there is truly a need.

Floor

It's good to have
your own floor.
Did it shake
or suffer
beneath you?
I don't
dance, but
I do pace
to and fro
and go about
my tasks.
I'm angry
now and then,
angry and
heavy on my foot;
there must still be
something
young in me,
young,
a wild horse
tugging at its reins.
And sometimes
the floor groans,
rattling my cupboards
and stove.

Acestes

The first arrow quivers in the mast,
another cuts the cord and frees the dove
which rising high falls for a third,
better-placed arrow.
Nonetheless, grey-haired Acestes,
draw your bow. You must!
Dare the shot, make your arrow catch fire – – –

Bertolt Brecht

Bertolt Brecht was a versatile fellow.
Playwright, actor, poet.
His poems were easy to grasp,
they stood on your stoop
like a pair of wooden clogs.

Everyday Life

The great storms
are behind you now.
Back then, you didn't ask
why you were born, where
you came from, or where you were going
– you were part of the storm,
the fire.
But you can find a way to live
in everyday life as well,
in our ordinary grey days:
plant your potatoes, rake leaves,
clear away the brush.
There is so much to ponder in this world
that one life is not enough.
After you're done with your tasks,
you can fry up some bacon
and read Chinese poetry.
Old Laërtes hacked back the brambles
and hoed the earth around his fig trees,
letting the heroes battle it out at Troy.

The Watcher

The watcher
waits for
that nibble
from below.
Will he hold?
Not to worry,
as long as the fish are small.
Frozen, he waits on the ice,
always he waits alone.
I like the watcher.
He shows us when it's biting out there.
That's all he can.

Signpost

Time flows,
whirls and turns,
blinds us –
Somewhere the signpost
stands firm.

Weathercock

The blacksmith beat
his comb and tail into shape,
then he was raised high,
saw the world anew,
felt many winds.
He was keen,
restless, cawed and
puffed his feathers
at each gust
– in the storm he stood straight,
neck stretched.
Till he rusted
stuck, skewed
to the north.
From where the wind
most often comes.

Executioner's Axe

The executioner's axe
is busy these days. There
a head falls,
and another,
silvery and solemn.
Who will get the axe
tomorrow?
You're safe. Never demanded anything.
You and the throng in the square are whipped to a frenzy.

Sword

The sword
cuts
when drawn,
if nothing else
– then air.

Arrow or Bullet

Arrows came before bullets.
That's why I prefer arrows.
The bullet flies many miles,
but its crack is terrible.
The arrow smiles.

No Cause for Worry

Mount Vassfjøro
has donned sackcloth and ashes
and pulled down its hood.
The other mountains bathe
in the evening sun; there's
no cause for worry.
Storms over the North Sea,
says the weather forecast.

Don't Use Sandpaper

Don't use sandpaper where a steady blade has cut.
Don't blaze a new ski trail where the old one crossed the mountains safely.
Don't take back words once said.
Words are dynamite, reaching both high and deep.
In that crack they blasted,
groundwater can rise.

Poem

If you can make a poem
a farmer finds worthwhile,
you should be happy.
A smith is hard to fathom.
The worst to please is the carpenter.

Old Poet Tries His Hand as a Modernist

He too was determined to try
these new stilts.
He's hoisted himself up,
strides warily as a stork.
Amazing how far-sighted he is.
He can even count his neighbor's sheep.

I Have Three Poems

I have three poems,
he said.
Who counts poems?
Emily tossed hers
into a trunk, I
don't believe she ever counted them.
She just spread open a tea-packet
and wrote a new one.
That was the right thing to do. A good poem
should smell of tea.
Or of raw earth and freshly split firewood.

The Bird Cliff

Perhaps you like being a bird cliff.
I understand, it's fine with a bird or two,
but to be this screeching crag of restless wings?
Your conceit and folly must have brought
this crowd of birds and made them
shit all over you.

What I Remember Best

What I remember best from childhood
is the wind.
Now there is no wind left.
No wind
and no birds.
What's in store for us?

Today I Saw

Today I saw
two moons,
a new moon
and an old moon.
I have a lot of faith in the new moon.
But I suppose it's just the old one.

Red Scar

This red scar in the mask?
Sure, it's ugly.
But quite useful:
this ram's horn,
radar screen,
bulldozer,
stump-puller,
car bumper
– it all depends
on whom
you have to face.

Rotting Tree Stump

Worms and fungus have
eaten away all his softness.
The hard remains, the tough
and the twisted. Knots and gnarls
still hold him up.

The Crag

This crag shows me his scars,
scouring marks and deep gouges where frost clawed.
Yet there were many days he drank the sun,
stroked by a mild wind.

In the Chicken Yard

In the chicken yard, you should
keep clear of
the cock and the boss hen
– don't blink,
don't take a step!
A mere nod from you
is a snake bite.

End of Summer

Foxgloves are ringing
their last red bells,
this evening wind strokes
forgotten grass.

Autumn

Autumn is coming.
The lilies stand
with broken swords,
the hunched grass
tells us
it is here!

They can turn the sun
and make the moon
into a scimitar.
And yet, my friend,
I still rule frost
and snow!

Blue Musicians

They stand there
embracing
music made
of what
they've inherited,
filling with blue wind
the space
before them.
Within that wind
they stand
and blow
– they're
just that blue wind.
They are
blue wind
until
– is there
anything left
of them?
There – those brass horns
weren't cackling, but
on the verge.
Eyes stare
after that
note,
which soars
as white
specks.

Today I Sensed

Today I sensed
that I'd made a good poem.
When I came outside, the birds were singing in my garden
and the sun was shining joyously over the Bergafjell.

When I Wake

When I wake, a black
raven's hacking at my heart.
Shall I never again awaken
to sea and stars, forests and night,
or a morning with birdsong?

They Yearn to Be Away

They yearn to be away
from this world – all of them.
The insect flutters,
and the worm sheds its soil.

Slot Machine

Insert your coin
– hear your quarter
bravely tossed about inside:
now it's rummaging in a pirate's chest,
now it's shaking the money tree,
now it'll be raining money,
now it's prying open the vault,
now popping the lock,
now the floodgates will open.
You wait. Uncertain.
Jingling.
Silence.
Nothing comes out.

When Autumn Comes

When autumn comes
when the cold comes
and evenings turn dark,
I sit by the fire
and hum my song
– this keeps anguish alive,
conjures forth glowing memories.

The Mirror

When I was young,
I'd look at myself in
the blacksmith's window.
Our heart sees itself
in God's mirror.
Which is smoky too.

In My Father's House

In my Father's house are many rooms,
and many are the doors leading in.
What stairway will you crawl up,
what tears will you shed,
what bell will you toll
– will you grab the maul or beat
your knuckles bloody?
Will they open only for
shouting horns and trumpet blasts?

There comes a moment
when the door swings on its hinges;
you never know whether
that moment will come again.
Odin lets go of your keel, and
"A Village Romeo and Juliet" sails
into heaven on a haystack!

Torch

The pine torch
knows much,
burns long
and bright,
can kindle others
and sees much.
But it takes no heed of this,
its flame is free.
The harsh smoke
stings nose
and eyes.
And afterwards
– I don't care
about thanks.

The Birch

He had noticed
one thing,
said Old Man Hallvor,
that the birch grows
only in the morning.
That sounds like nonsense.
I believe we grow while sleeping.

Wild Rose

There are songs of roses.
I want to sing of the thorns
and the root – how it grips
the rock as firmly as
a girl's slender hand.

Scythe

I am so old
I keep to the scythe.
Quietly it sings in the grass,
and my thoughts roam free.
There is no pain,
says the grass,
to fall for the scythe.

The Cat

The cat is
sitting in the
farmyard when you come.
Speak a little with the cat. More than anyone
he senses what's really going on.

Morning on the Fjord

The local steamer cuts
the still black water,
hull-plates turn
toward the green shore.

Green Apples

Summer was cold and rainy.
The apples are green and full of scabs,
yet I pick and sort them
and stack the crates in my cellar.
Green apples are better than none at all.
My farm lies at sixty-one degrees north.

Stettarbekken

Once again I can see the brook, Stettarbekken.
He's long been obscured by the spruce on Sjur's farm,
but I see now he still finds the strength
to make his way down that steep cliff.

It Is That Dream

It is the dream we carry
that something wonderful will happen,
that it must happen –
that time will open,
that our hearts may open,
that doors shall open,
and the mountain shall open
that springs will gush forth –
that our dream will open,
and that one morning we'll glide
into a cove we didn't know.

Ask the Wind
Spør vinden
1971

Overleaf: Hauge sharing a philosophical exchange with a Fjord Horse, 1975. Photo: Bodil Cappelen. (Archives of the Olav H. Hauge Centre, Ulvik, Norway.)

Excerpts from Hauge's Journals – through autumn 1971

4 July 1966

Summer – The evenings are long. To go out at night, visit the hotels down by the fjord, order a coffee or a beer, and sit there conversing with tourists or villagers. That's a suitable thing to do at ten-ish in the evening. The whole world comes here now. Why not interact with them? I shall consider that. Invite along Sigurd and buy him a beer at the café. Many times he's made food when I've visited him. Do it tomorrow. And remember to get a haircut. Relax a little! You're too bound up in habits.

Do you dare?
You must dare. You must.

23 November

Books from my publisher. Three copies of *Droplets on the Eastern Wind.* Yes, no fancy cover. That's good.

Outsiders – They stood outside respectable society, our "culture". Blake, Verlaine, Baudelaire, Rimbaud, Hopkins, Dickinson – yes, and we almost forgot Poe, he did as well. And Corbière.

15 January 1967

Chinese Poetry – In its forceful simplicity, its clarity as well as hidden meaning, I understand that nothing can compare to Chinese or Japanese poetry. Many of our best writers have received strong impressions from that source. Brecht's encounter with Waley's translations liberated him as a poet. (European poetry is too ornate, contains too many flourishes.)

A Good Poem – Today I came across a good poem: "A Foreign Wind Has Stirred the Horseman of Tai" by Li Po. What a poem! The translator is Arthur Waley.

3 April

Large windows and grand poems – I like neither.

Rather a small opening in the wall
with wavy green glass.

6 November

A wind-still autumn day, fine weather. It's beautiful. Started reading *Travel Sketches* by the Japanese poet Bashō How concentrated, how magnificent he writes, gradually making poetry. Simple little nature poems, haiku. No one has traveled with a lighter backpack. But he follows the wind. He has no lofty opinion of himself or his poetry, nor about the diary he keeps. He encounters poets, monks and priests, visits temples and holy places. He is glad all the same: "My joy was great when I encountered anyone with the slightest understanding of artistic elegance."

Yes, that's the man who wrote these beautiful words:

Only for morning glories
I open my door –
During the daytime I keep it
Tightly barred.

But his masterpiece is *The Narrow Road to the Deep North.* I'll write more on that. Here is a poem by Bashō:

Under the same roof
We all slept together
Concubines and I –
Bush-clover and moon.

Finished reading *The Narrow Road to the Deep North.* A fine book. Poetry. Such humble means, so simple!

This Is Bashō

With a bit of madness in me,
Which is poetry,

I plod the Chikusai
Among the wails of the wind.

16 April 1969

Held in high regards by the ladies. When I came to Bergen Sunday evening, no less than four women offered me lodging for the night. I was exhausted and weak and glad I managed to make my way to a hotel room. Women, they're strange creatures. One of them was young, had just finisher her studies in French philology, and was quite pretty. I regret that now. I should have accepted her invitation.

25 February 1970

An unexpected letter from Bodil Strømsted, who lives at Staubø. Says she's a weaver. And married to Finn Strømsted. A fresh and joyous letter! From a person I've never seen or heard of.

Dear Olav Hauge *10 April '70*

Thank you so much for the books! I love them! The poems are strong and fragrant, so I'm going to try to translate some of them. I feel close to you. I am travelling now, and must leave again, so I dash off this brief note, and send you this duck, upon whom much rain has fallen. It is my favourite duck.

With admiration
Yours Robert Bly

28 October

Stomach ache. I'm sitting still and reading too much. Some sunny weather today. Cold. Snow on the mountains. Should have written Kari Lie. Should have written Eileen Ørbeck. And to Siri Endresen as well. Did write to Anne Vallevik at Stend today. That's a lot of women. Astrid Noreng deserves a word as well; she asked to see me again this spring. And Edel Bjorstad wrote a letter from Spain a while back. Perhaps I'll see Bodil Strømsted soon, if she comes as she said she will.

God help me!

10 December

Days pass. Wrote letters. It takes time to write letters. Today I received two (written the same date) from Bodil Strømsted at Staubø. She must be a strange person. She weaves. Knows all sorts of things.

She's knitting me a vest, she says. Well, well. And Bitten Dahl has written me from Dombås. She wants to rent a house here this summer. Well, well.

11 December

A package from Bodil Strømsted. She has knitted me a sweater, nice and warm!

These women!

2 January 1971

Yesterday and today I wrote a letter to Bodil Strømsted, a long letter! She writes so warmly and vividly, while my letters are dull and dry.

This last year has seen a lot of letter writing, especially to ladies. They're more fun to write to as well. I should have known that before! …

Radio. Play. Dance. I dance on the floor. It's fun, does me good! I sing a little, too.

15 January

A letter from Bodil Strømsted. She is weaving a tapestry she calls "Asteroid," she says. I barely know what that is; small planets that are orbiting somewhere between Mars and Jupiter, supposedly fifteen-hundred of them, of irregular shape and irregular orbits. The closest one is called Eros. It will be a sparkling tapestry!

28 October

Today I started thinking about that poem by Jan Erik Vold:

> What does the light do
> in the birch trees?
> In the birch trees
> the light is looking about.

The first two lines are easy enough. But notice how with his last two lines he creates space, a wonderfully luminous space. That's poetry.

Into the light birch leaves. Take notice: there, precisely there, the light is looking about.

What is a Poem? – No one knows. And that's good, because as long as they don't know, they keep at it – and they keep wondering. How should a poem be?

No one knows. And that's good. That's when we keep writing and wondering.

To make a poem is one of those impossible things. Impossible for God. Some things are. And that's how it should be. As long as it is, people keep trying to write poetry.

What is poetry for one person is nothing of the sort for another.

Overnight the Grass Turns Green

Overnight the grass has turned green.
A bird dares to sing,
the mist rises,
and the sun climbs above the snowy mountains.
From mornings long ago joy
faintly beats its copper shield.

T'ao Ch'ien

Should T'ao Ch'ien
come to visit someday, I will
show him my cherry and apple trees;
I hope he'll come in the spring
when they're in bloom. Then we'll sit in the shade
with a glass of cider, perhaps I'll show him
a poem – if I can find one he'd like.
The dragons that blazed across the sky, trailing smoke and poison,
soared more quietly in his day, and more birds sang.
There's nothing here he wouldn't understand.
More than ever he'd want to retire
to a small garden like mine.
But I'm not sure his conscience would let him.

Time To Harvest

These mild sunny days of September.
It's time to harvest. There are still bushes ripe
with lingonberries in the woods, rosehips reddening
along the stone walls, nuts ready to fall,
clusters of blackberries gleaming in the thicket,
thrushes searching for the last red currants
and wasps sucking on the sweet plums.
At dusk I put the ladder away and hang
my basket in the shed. Already there is
a sprinkle of new snow on the patches
that never quite melted on the mountain.
Lying in bed, I hear the fishermen
head out for brisling. All night they will
glide back and forth with their floodlights
searching the fjord.

The Storm Has Been Here and Swept the Doorstep Clean of Rubbish

The storm has been here
and swept the doorstep clean of rubbish,
night is gone,
the weathervane screeches,
people are amazed their houses are still standing.
The ocean tossed restlessly, throwing
sandy shipwrecks onto the shore,
the woods are fleeing along with the clouds,
– even the oaks of Jæren were forced to lie down.
Young men who yearned for adventure, and good seamen too,
sailed in their bunks under Captain MacWhirr.
A car strives to stay on the road across the mountain plateau.
Sheep seek shelter between the boulders.
People living at the head of the fjord huddle inside;
they'll empty their ash-drawers another day.

Silence

It's a strange thing,
when we get together, we tend to talk
about ourselves (surely we've done
something worthy, we've heard
compliments from people
in the know, and no doubt we
have suffered wrongs) there is
a pressure on
our heart
that needs release.

But we stay silent. Perhaps sounds come,
but our thoughts circle
around these other things.
The testimonies we have prepared
(and there are many),
are locked away in a safe
where they earn interest.

The Salmon Weir

Not much left of the river, it sneaks
down like a thief between those rocks.
But we still see the old riverbed:
polished rockfaces, pools filled with
sand and brushwood and old stumps,
and a salmon weir left dry. Its wood is
still firm, bolted to the mountain in its
chosen spot. There the water rushed
past slippery logs and crafty sluice-
ways when the river ran low,
the salmon ladder itself a narrow gap
where rapids ran green – now the salmon
weir stands useless on a heap of stones.

Lone Pine

Plenty of space, here you were able
to reach high and spread your crown
wide.

But you'll stand alone.
When the storms come, you have
no one to lean on.

The Lighthouse

The lighthouse blinks in its friendly way,
convinced we have returned safely.
Swells lift us. The engine beats steadily
beneath these worn planks, the reek of oil
is familiar. Friendly blinks follow
our boat though we're in calmer waters now
– the darkness a soft velvet; on both sides
mountains silent and somber, we know
they will yield, let the fjord slip inward.
Why do I think of the Prince of Aquitaine,
of black sun, the grieving blue tone of a lute,
and snuffed-out stars?

Behind us, far out there, the beacon
slowly turns under its helmet and blinks its warning.
Light shafts reveal the strife of black reefs,
the deadly row of skerries grins in the yellow light.

I grab a handful of grain, some leaves, a few twigs,
and offer them for the sake of this poem.
Our boat scarcely has enough ballast stone.

The Cropped Hazel

A cropped hazel stands
in the stone heap where the road
turns toward my yard.
A scrawny self-sown
hazel grove.

One night I come home,
there are two rowans.
They must have stood there
a long time, crooked and weathered.
It's autumn. Their leaves
are rust-red.

Suddenly a tossing
and singing – two
green poplars soar
sky high
on each side
of the gate.

In the dawn light
I go out and look. I liked
those old rowans.
Now there is nothing
other than that
cropped hazel.

The Big Apple Tree Outside My Window

I chopped down the big apple tree outside my window,
which was blocking the view. In the summer,
my living room was dim and gloomy, and besides,
the wholesalers no longer wanted
that kind of apple.
I think of what my father
might have said – he liked
that apple tree.
But I chopped it down.

There's more light now, I can
see out over the fjord and more
of the life around me;
the house is now in full
view, shows
more of itself.

I don't want to admit it, but I miss that apple tree.
Things are not the same here. It gave shelter against the wind and
good shade, letting patches of sunlight slip through its branches
onto my table. At night I often lay listening
to the rustling leaves. And those apples – none
were finer in the spring, with their spicy tang.
It hurts every time I see that stump. When it gets spongy,
I'll break it from the ground and hack it into firewood.

Dead Tree

The magpie has flown;
she won't build in a dead tree.

A Sunny Day in March

Even the weathercock turns toward the sun
on such a day. It must be spring. The cat has found
shelter outside the cellar wall. He may be asleep, but
he has fluffed up his fur and tucked under his paws.
A fly is tempted out from a crack
in the warm plank wall – and it starts
buzzing. Soon it stiffens. Much too cold.

The Dugout

A large log became visible in the sandy shore
when they drained the water.
There was something strange about it;
as we dug it out we realized it was a boat.
And what a beautiful boat it once had been, with
elegant lines – that's where
the rower sat, and there were the oarlocks.

I suppose it had drifted off
or been left there by a fisherman,
although none can say how long ago.
Now it lay there, wet and gleaming black.
It was beautiful, indeed, and we decided
to fetch it by boat another day.
We left it lying on the sand in the sunlight.
When we came back, we didn't speak, didn't look
at that hollowed, cracked vessel
as we towed it home over the lake.

A Farm Had the Bow and Arrow as Its Mark

I have death in my head
and in my greedy barbs,
sings the arrow.

I send that arrow
from my string,
quavers the bow.

Who draws that bow
lest it be me
– the strong arm?

Who spots the bird,
aims that arrow?
asks the eye.

I tense the arm
and guide that eye,
claims the will.

Aim – let fly!
Mine is the poison
that kills, mutters
the hunter's zeal.

That bird is mine,
often I see him,
reminds the dream.

And the bird vanished
on shy wings
into the dark woods.

Looking Over the Scythes Before Cutting Grass

Used scythes
stay shiny,
never rust, yet
I see these too wear out.
Which is best – rusting unused in the toolbox
or worn out by whetstone and rocky meadow?

The Trapping Pit

Just a hollow
in the ground now,
sunken,
stones have fallen in,
earth and leaves
have filled
it up.
You pause a bit,
it's not really
worth noticing,
a reindeer hoof
would hardly
trip over it
– not now.

William Blake

What trumpet is this
resounding so clearly
through the morning sun?
What voice is this
calling
so strong
and bold?
Tiger and angel
– in secret
your fire glows,
your wings
still folded,
your gait so light.
Long have I heard you,
bright and clear
on this Earth,
among hoarse horns
and braying bulls.

Gérard de Nerval

A body burned
to exhaustion – can't he
swing from a lamppost?

There remains
the glow in faithful eyes,
and this voice from a heart
that has slept its diamond sleep.

The Old Poet Has Made a Verse

The old poet has made a verse.
And he's happy, happy as a cider bottle
in the spring after it's sent up
a fresh bubble and is
about to pop its cork.

The Prince

It's all behind him now,
in a vast darkness:
the realm he ruled,
life. He's done
with that now,
and he'll say
nothing about
that terrifying
light.

He sits there. A sack of bones
in a black cape. His hands
are still – he's blind.
Although he sees, not
backward (that darkness
is his own) but
forward,
for you, and he
asks you just
as he was
asked:

Do you exist?
You know
why?
He says
nothing.

Ask.

The Last Spider

Above Sveig Pasture,
 so high
  the heather was

about to give up, I came
 upon the last
  spider, she

was hung
 in her own web.

Summer had been
 cold, scant with
  moths and meager
   with mosquitoes,

and the flies
 had stayed where
  things are fatter.

Yes, I came round
 that juniper thicket
  and there

hung the spider
 trembling
  in the autumn wind.

Leaf-Huts and Snow-Houses

There's not much to
these poems, just
a few words, piled together
at random.
Still, I take
pleasure in
making them; it's as if
for a short while
I have a house.
I recall the leaf-huts
we built of branches
when we were kids;
we would crawl inside, sit
listening to the rain,
alone in that wild place,
feeling the raindrops
on our noses and in our hair
– or snow-houses at Christmas,
we'd crawl inside,
seal the hole with
a burlap sack,
light a candle, be there
through the cold evenings.

Read Lu Chi and Make a Poem

Read Lu Chi and make a poem.
He doesn't say how it should be.
Many had painted an oak before.
Nevertheless Munch painted an oak.

Here I have Lived

Here I have lived for more than an age of man.
Years have sailed past with wind and stars
in the high rigging.
Trees and birds have settled in,
but I have not.

I See You've Learned

I like
how you
use so
few words,
few words and
short sentences
that drift
down the page
like a rain-shower
filled with
light and
air.

I see you've
learned to stack a
woodpile in the forest;
it's good
to build
it tall
so it'll dry;
in a long and low pile
the wood will rot.

One Poem a Day

I want to write one poem a day,
every day.
That should be easy enough.
Browning kept at it for a long time,
and he was rhyming as well,
counting the meter
with his bushy brows.
So, one poem a day.
Something strikes you,
something happens,
something grabs your attention.
– I get out of bed. Dawn comes.
The best of intentions.
The bullfinch flies out from the cherry tree
where he's been stealing buds.

Sogn

Odin always rode
high above Sogn,
his ravens came back
scorched;
the raven
from Skjær
was even blacker.
"Something's wrong,"
roared Thor,
the crags echoing
his words.
The Stone of Bele was green;
I know why Sogn
will not sing
– there's song
where Eggjum
chanted!
"Too tall,"
they said of that
Fridtjov in bronze.
The smiths
turn
their tong.

Old Tiger

The old tiger
slinks through the grass
searching
for prey.
Shall he dare
the leap?
Can he,
will he reach?

Is that coiled power
gone, claws and teeth
dulled?
Has he hearkened
what the monkey says,
the birds that mock him
from the trees?

The prey is majestic!
Holding stars
between its huge horns,
it comes
to the watering hole
at dusk.

A Letter Is Coming

A letter is coming.
And I'll be happy.
A wave of sorrow
sweeps me up the hill.

In the Parker Pen

There are many poems in the Parker pen – a whole mile full,
and even more in the inkwell,
mile after mile of them. Papers
arrive in my mailbox: bills, brochures, forms
to be filled out.
I face the future with confidence.

Don't Stand There Shouting at the Mountain

Don't stand there
shouting at the mountain.
Of course it's true
what you say,
so true it echoes
in fools and tools.
Go inside that mountain
make your smithy there
build your forge there
heat your iron there,
sing while you hammer!
We hear you,
hear you well,
we know what you're at.

Raking Leaves

There wasn't much today.
But I did gather
some debris
brought here
by the wind.
Maybe it was
someone else's
or meant
for another,
I don't know.
Mustn't steal!
That's what
I often heard
as a young lad.

Cold Day

The sun squints
behind the frozen
mountain range.
The mercury
crawls lower
and lower
– our warmth
curls up
in a tiny
pocket.
I burn firewood sparingly,
keep my verse
short.

Midwinter. Snow

Midwinter. Snow.
I throw out bread crusts for the birds.
And I lose no sleep over that.

After Winter

The forest is silent beneath the stars.
In this calm after winter.

Not yet suspense,
no great excitement.
Shall the spring star or
winter darkness own it?

Springs flow onto the forest floor.
The thrush has come.
Through the snow crust
sparse grass stirs in the wind.

Coming Home

Magpies explode from the front porch.
Cats scatter from the corners.
The key is still where I left it.

Dead flies on the windowsills.
The kettle cold and full of coffee grounds.
In the drawer a hardened crust.
Tall goosefoot peep into the windows.

Snowmen in the Green Hayfield

No one expected snow this early.
Kids brought out their sleds, made snowmen, built huts.
Today it's sunny and warm again. The snowmen
stand alone weeping in the green hayfield.

Looking at the Postmark on Your First Letter

I look at the postmark on your first letter.
A month has passed since it came.
Since then you've haunted this house,
enticed me, called me, shifting
from Até to a green Erinyes.
Today I got your photograph:
a pale girl sitting alone on some logs
by the darkening sea.

I Aim a Little High

For an arrow to hit the mark, it can't
veer much in its flight. That's why the good archer
allows for wind and distance.
When I aim at you, I aim a little high.

Still You're Riding At His Side

Still you're riding
at his side
with the setting sun
in the mane,
sparks and beating hoofs
echo through
the desolate mountains
– still you're
riding at his side,
through rainfall
in the wind
that stiffens
on this trail
that descends,
steeper and steeper,
down, down to the very bottom.

I know no more,
and the autumn night is falling.

Woe to He Who Gets Old

Poor old thing
and smitten with love!
See the glow in his cheeks
his eye gleaming
with dead dreams!
An old birch will soon
be splotched by red rot.

An Order Has Gone Out

The order has gone out
that all the world's diamonds
be counted in the census and
assigned to cut glass.

He's a Man Just Like You

You held him in regard
as long as you didn't
know him and
grasp what
he was
up to.

When you did,
you lost respect.
He's a man,
and just like you,
trying to be
a peacock.

Deadweight

Are you keen on this
space flight, or are you
one of these deadweights,
anchored to the ground saying
this will never fly?

Nothing to be done about deadweights.
They just stand there.
You can weigh them, they won't
raise their voice at that.
But they'll stick to their stance,
just as unyielding, just as cool.

They're the ones
who really know
how heavy things are.

Horses and Tramps

Horses and tramps look for
roadside water-troughs.
What use have they
for gas stations?

Strange Fish

Trust people?
You quickly see
what strange
fish they are
– now green,
now black,
now blue.
It should be
the light, the riverbed
and the current that
make them change color.

That Man

That old jacket
on a hook in the shed,
and the worn shoes,
I know that
man.

I've moved him
to another peg,
to the other corner.
He was in the way.
But I don't have
the heart to
throw him
out.

Wind and Weather

The wind has stirred up storm.
"Hold out, children!"
says the weather.

Christmas Sheaf

Your Christmas
sheaf isn't
worth much
this year
– grain's all shed,
moldy and green
on the floor of
your barn.

But you
raise your sheaf
high on a stake, and
you expect thanks
from the birds
as well as
Our Lord.

I Drift

I drift
with the wind, with the waves.
I've clawed my way onto a beam
and I'm proud of its carvings.

There Are Omens

There are omens:
winds, spirits, birds.
And swinging doors.

Who
did I see
in the glass
when you came in?

The door swings shut.
Neither of us says a word.

You Don't Hang Your Hat on a Sunbeam

You insist on
firm ground beneath
your feet, something

to grasp,
your thought
doesn't dare

let go.
It's like a child, who
doesn't trust himself but

without fail fumbles
for a grip.
You don't

hang your hat
on a sunbeam.
You were late

learning to swim,
anxious about flying,
and feel safe only

when you're on foot.

December Moon 1969

He hides his steel
in a silver sheath.
There's blood on the blade.

New Year 1970

A pastor's wife in black
has come unannounced to the farm.
And a yellow wolf.

I Lose Myself to Daydreams

I lose myself to daydreams
in this furthest hayfield,
here amidst hogweed
and bracken.
Round the tussock grass
float butterflies
more beautiful than any
bird of paradise
– I am a child again
and I'm away,
at one with
the fragrant grass
and soaring
clouds
– until
a wind gust
shakes the top
of a lone fern that
towers like a pine
and ants
creep
under my clothes.

Dance

In all things, now, there is a restless energy.
The sunlight dances, the stars
flow, the fields flow, the grass
dances, there's dance in the wasps' nest, dance
in women and men,
cars, airplanes and wires
are restless, my oven
and my kettle
are restless,
the restless cat dances
– dance, dance, dance
all we touch flows and dances, says Olai.
That's why he's standing there in rubber boots
digging deep to reach
clay and cold water.

Dieu de la Danse
(Vaslav Nijinsky)

God appeared again, in the body of a dancer.
He danced life and death, war and peace.

The great sculptor said:
I cannot carve you
nor draw you.
For you are perfect.

And the dancer hung a cross around his neck and
walked out amongst the warring people
and said: "I am God."
"I am love."
"I am peace."
And he cried
for the world.

That's when they shut him away,
until his dancing flame
died down.

Then they could
draw him and sculpt him,
and his message
became words
in a book.

The Steamroller

He sounds his warning at the bend,
comes toward you in the grey light of dawn
fiery horns
blinking from his forehead –
rolling heavily, rolling forth with great authority,
smoothing out the asphalt path you must follow.

Everyone must stay on that asphalt strip,
these conveyor belts that carry us
from the maternity ward to the crematorium.

Not By Car – Nor Plane

Not by car, nor plane,
not haysled
nor old clunker
– not by Elijah's chariot of fire!

You won't get any farther than Bashō.
He got there on foot.

The Sun and Almighty Aren't the Only Ones Who See What's Happening

The sun and Almighty are no longer the only ones who see what's
happening in this world. Even we who live in this village have an eye on
the battlefields and the ghettoes, and the moon and the Hong Kong
stock exchange. We see whether smoke is rising again from
the arms factories, whether Napoleon's sarcophagus

is undisturbed, whether the Statue of Liberty still lifts her torch
at the entrance to New York harbor. This evening we peer into
the court of a Parisian castle; crystal chandeliers hang from the ceiling,
the walls are covered in damask, princes and politicians roam
among gilded frames, and stiff-backed chairs face the table

which is heaped with treaties and documents, dictaphones, gold
fountain pens, flowers and flags. Surely these border disputes ought
to be resolved quickly, but we forget that for two hundred years
our own families have been fighting with neighbors encroaching
on our mountain pastures, that we complained and sent the matter

to arbitration, had it brought before parliament, asked for a local
inquest, demanded official boundaries be drawn up by the proper
authorities, appealed and lost in court, not because the people
who live on that neighboring farm are worth all the effort, but
because we insist that we're in the right. And we ask each other
what in the world are the Americans doing in Vietnam?

Even I, a woodcarver, have a firm opinion on that matter.

Looking at an Old Mirror

On the front a mirror.
On the back a picture of the Garden of Eden.

A strange whim
from the old master glazier.

From the War

A bullet clattered onto the floor in my hallway.
I weighed it in my hand.
It had passed through glass and
two timber walls.
I had no doubt it could kill.

Arctic Mother, Finnmark 1944

Stormy seas and snow-swept plains and cold
seem almost homely and cherished after this:
Singing green soldiers, in the shadow of black eagles, came
and unleashed their yellow wolves of burning flames
on our pauper lands. Hopeless it seemed
for autumn snowflakes to hide
those charred remains. The unwilling wind swept away
the snow, tore open the wounds, howling
with the survivors' laments. Our hopes
keep dying – but at least our distress
holds madness at bay. In such times
as these, prayers are strong.

Child, you don't realize
the world you've come to,
you cannot understand
your mother's dark tear.

(On an etching by Kaare Espolin Johnson)

Swine

Strange how this state of mind lingers
from that first wooden sword and tomahawk!
I am a peaceful man and a coward,
but I confess I've often enjoyed
the battlefield. With all my experience, I should
know well the art of war and the use of weapons
– stone axe, poisoned arrow, spear and saber,
catapult, cannon and tank.
I pass through the wilderness with The Ten Thousand; I am
that dervish-shadow clutching rifle and *burnous*
riding with Lawrence across the burning sand;
grey as sharp old steel, my memories circle
the fortresses and siege ladders; in green armor heavy with blood
I peer with Tintoretto out over the jagged walls.
Marching armies, drums, banners and vanguards!
In their tents, commanders pore over maps; the grasses yield
as Genghis Khan's horsemen and yaks sweep across the steppes . . .
With Hugo I taste defeat at Waterloo, though I also
refresh my memories alongside Fabrice. Facing the storm of
steel in Flanders I tell jokes; with the executioners
I raise my rifle at the prison wall; I am there
at Borodino and Sevastopol, at clay-grey Verdun,
eye blinded, Bierce, and nerves numb as death spreads.
It is evening after Gettysburg. In a valley
I come across a flock of black swine rooting
in the stomachs of the dead and injured – they raise
their crimson muzzles and look suspiciously
from the edge of this circle of light
falling from my reading lamp.

Ask the Wind

Ask the wind,
and best the gentle breeze.
He travels far
and often comes back
with a good answer.

Gleanings
Janglestrå
1980

Overleaf: Rolf Jacobsen (foreground) and Olav H. Hauge were the two pre-eminent Norwegian poets of the 20th century – one writing in *Bokmål,* the other in *Nynorsk.*

"Never has this much poetry been published. Much of it is junk. But above them all towers Rolf Jacobsen whose debut was *Earth and Iron* in 1933. That book of poems will endure." – Olav H. Hauge.

(Archives of the Olav H. Hauge Centre, Ulvik, Norway.)

Excerpts from Hauge's Journals – through autumn 1980

16 June 1972

Fine sunny weather. Saw a butterfly today, sitting on a raspberry leaf. Dark red. Must have been a copper, a *Lycaenini,* even though they're not supposed to appear until July. I'm writing this down, because butterflies have become rare now. Yes, rare! Butterflies, there were lots of them before. These days you stop in amazement when you spot one.

A letter from Bodil Cappelen. She has reclaimed her maiden name, after using her husband's (Strømsted) for twenty years. Yes, she always writes such joyous letters.

The Wheel

I am a spoke
– a spoke in the wheel.
One of many.
Jutting
from the hub,
propped against the wheel rim,
which is propped against me.
All who lean against the rim
jut from the hub,
together making one wheel.
When that wheel turns
we are one wheel.
When standing still,
we dream,
every spoke dreams,
that we shoot beyond the rim
poking our
ends into
eternity.

23 August

Not only Robert Bly has written about the morning glory. Chigo of Kaya has written a renowned haiku, which in English sounds like this:

> Ah! Morning-glory!
> The bucket taken captive!
> I begged for water.

Suzuki writes beautifully about this poem. No one has written as beautifully about haiku as Suzuki in his *Zen and the Japanese Culture*. A wonderful book! Look at what he writes about Bashō!

Haiku cannot be understood without knowing Zen.

Should have been traveling today, but Suzuki and what he writes about Japanese poetry keeps me home. Besides, it's raining.

29 August

Sunday morning, good weather. Decided to take a trip to Lærdal.

> Only for morning glories
> I open the door –
> During the daytime I keep it
> Tightly barred.
>
> –Bashō

Aftenposten printed one of my poems the other day. But does that wealthy newspaper bother to pay me? Hardly! No doubt they believe the honor should be sufficient. That attitude is typical of major publications. Just as Amlie, the local pastor, always said that being allowed to work for a priest was a great thing; he had a farm, and he was always in need of workers to lend him a hand.

> Start the day
> without a poem?
> Since I don't pray,
> that's the least
> I can do.

I search for
something to write about,
and I recall the hare
sitting outside my kitchen window
one spring morning.

I have often noticed:
when your suffering is greatest
the song flows best.

What does the arrow see?
The target.

Grief squeezes
your heart like
a fist the sponge.
Feel how refreshing
and easy that was!

Pen and paper
and ink
are apt
tools.

Lots of apples to pick
this autumn. But many
poems, too.
Tinder and kindling,
I should make a poem
about that,
so I'll remember them.

These little
grasshopper songs.

Mountains expect you
and friends as well,
and poems in
a calm evening pool.

No poem
today. I have walked
blindly, nothing has
lit a song in my heart.

29 September 1972

Letter from Bodil Cappelen. She is traveling with *Epos,* the book ship, along the coast of Møre & Romsdal. A refreshing, well-written letter.

17 January 1973

I've cut down trees around the orchard. Mostly rowan. It's amounting to quite a pile; I chop off the branches and twigs as I go, and drag them up to my courtyard. Good to be working. No snow. Read a bit.

A long letter from Bodil Cappelen. She's sent me an Emily Dickinson poem she's translated. Hard for me to comment. She doesn't convey the verse and meter, merely the content. That can be good as well.

In his translations, Robert Bly has shown that this is possible. But someone who knows Emily might not appreciate that approach, won't recognise the poems. The rhythm, especially the rhythm. The tone is lost; rhymes matter less – they can be rather awkward in Emily's poems. But you need the rhythm! The tone!

23 March

A letter from the Norwegian Book Club. They invite me to edit an anthology they're planning to publish. Poems about love! Norwegian as well as foreign poems can be included, in translation of course. I wonder who on their poetry committee suggested asking me. I see it as a good jest. For me to edit a collection of love poems! That would be quite something. Yes, I'm sure I would be able to put together such a collection. But I have no intention of taking on the task, even though they're offering me five-thousand kroner for the job. A bad joke.

24 March

Nice, sunny weather. Trimmed the apple trees. Read a little. A variety. Rexroth's excellent translations from Japanese. He's recreating the poem, as I understand it. Strange! However much I read, I seem to appreciate these poems from the Chinese and Japanese most of all.

27 March

Picked up the twigs lying about in the garden. It was quite a mess. But afterwards it tastes great with a meal, and a rest does me good! I feel sorry for people who don't have any sound physical work to do.

I wrote to the Norwegian Book Club, informing them that I won't be editing their anthology of love poetry. Love! Sure, I've heard about it and read about it, and I've felt the fever a few times as well; but I can't claim to be experienced in its deep mysteries, and the editor of such a collection should be. Sure, I could gather a beautiful bouquet of love poems. I would start with Sappho, include a few by Petrarch and Dante (from the *Vita Nuova*), continues with the troubadours, throw in some Chinese and Japanese poems – and then tackle the usual European literature.

Then there is Nordic poetry, and plenty to choose from! Yes, I would be able to fill such a book with poems!

5 May

There was a lot of Cranesbill (*Geranium pratense*) in the meadow before we ploughed. Now it has grown back. They're such beautiful flowers.

Joy. Reading poems by Verlaine, I am filled with joy, a calm fine joy. Melancholy, good satire, honesty, humor. And such wonderful language! And this music! We experience that same joy reading the poems of Hardy, although in a different way. There's more oak, more farmer in him.

But there is something sincere and persuasive. Robert Frost has it as well.

14 January 1974

My mother turned one-hundred and one yesterday. That's a respectable age! Few people live that long. That's a lot of days.

"To believe in immortality is one thing, but it is first needful to believe in life." – Robert Louis Stevenson

25 March

Henry Miller: Tropic of Capricorn – Been reading a book by Miller; if you've read them all, they're all variations on the same theme. One shouldn't take Miller literally. He sees the world and experiences it as though in a state of sexual delirium, and as known, in such a condition our minds and morals sleep and madness takes over. But what a thrill sometimes!

Miller: anarchistic sexual delirium. But still a rebellion against the decay of modern civilization, an exposure of its humbug. Never did the American way of life have a harsher critic.

25 May

Sunny. Slightly cooler. Sprayed the plum trees to protect them against mites.

The blossoms have fallen off the lilacs, one month earlier than usual. I see that it's forty years since I started my journals. There are forty-two notebooks; not too much written each year. They are otherwise quite worthless, seen as literature.

12 June

Left Oslo on 4 June. Stayed in Skien for three days, with Emil Stang who is married to Jarbjørg.

A meeting at Venstøm on the evening of 6 June. Saw the new Ibsen House in Skien. The bust of Henrik Ibsen himself stood in a glass cupboard in the city museum, his back toward you as you might expect.

I must have mentioned to Bodil Cappelen that I was going to Venstøp. And she came to the meeting there. Greeted her in the courtyard when we came. She walked so lightly, tall and slender, wearing a long deerskin coat, like the Indians use. *Deerfoot*, I thought, as we stood under the huge ash tree later. I hadn't seen her before, but she has been writing to me for four years, many wondrous letters. Now she is forty-four. Still beautiful. But she looked like someone had hurt her.

In the evening, many of us gathered at Emil Stang's. Bodil and I sat in a corner. The others thought that strange, because Jarbjørg announced loudly that I had to talk some with the others who were present as well. Bodil stayed with Thorsen and his wife, who live in Skien. In the morning, Thorsen came to pick me up for breakfast. Bodil followed me to the bus, which left at eleven.

20 November

A letter from Robert Bly is like receiving a letter from one of the Metaphysical Poets; even the handwriting is similar. He says that Anne Sexton is dead, a suicide, like Sylvia Plath. She was born in 1928 and was a fine poet. In the few poems that I have, she speaks much of death.

Bodil is wise and full of insight. She went through some of my translations when she was here, offered criticism. Very few critics have as good judgment as she. I was overwhelmed, for it was well done and it did not paint my work in a negative light. If only I had met her earlier! She wanted to come here four or five years ago, but I always ignored those suggestions. How dumb I was! I met her for the first time in Skien this spring.

27 November

Bodil writes that she is getting a divorce. She wants to move here. Well, this is an unexpected turn of events. I am not surprised that she has chosen divorce, living as she has. But does she know whether I can have her? It seems impossible; I have accepted the idea that I would be alone. She says I need her when I get old. True enough, but that she should tie herself down in this way, young and healthy as she is. I feel sorry for her; I suppose she has nowhere to move to. Unfortunate. Bodil is a fine person, I have no doubt of that.

29 November

Went to Voss yesterday. Had an infection in a tooth.

Been sitting inside. Reading.

I am sixty-six years old. And then join hands with someone so young (Bodil is forty-four), how is that going to go? Soon I will be old, while she is in her prime. I will get help and support if I become feeble, that's true. But to accept help in that way? I don't think it's right. I suppose it makes sense from an economic point of view. She, too, has a modest income from her weaving and writing and lecture tours and the like. But my life would be turned upside down. Habits run deep. But if she *really* wants to come here, so be it.

21 December

Letter from Bodil. She wrote six pages, bless her! And she writes well. And she understands poetry. Translation, too. No, Bodil is sharp. She has spent a lot of time with good artists, and you learn from that.

23 December

Wrote to Bodil. How glad I am for every word from her!

Third Day of Christmas

Letter from Bodil. She writes so vividly. And she is happy, she says. Busy working on new tapestries and new articles. She will be back here in February, when she is making a tour of the folk high schools in Hordaland county.

I think of Bodil. Bodil came to me needing solace and help. I cannot turn her away, not as long as there is something I can do for her. Bodil, she is in my thoughts all the time now.

It's unusual for me to have someone to exchange ideas with, someone I can trust and who has the heart to embrace them, to understand. Certainly I have known people, written letters, spoken with people. But was there anyone with whom I could truly trust? No, not until now. Bodil.

4 January 1975

I don't care for electric heating. In the morning, the first thing I do is to light a fire in the oven and add some good split birch. As soon as the fire is going, my living room is quite pleasant.

"The poor Bedouin's carpet." I have had that poem lying about for some time. Today I came across it again. Perhaps I can make it amount to something, now that I have a weaver for a sweetheart. And it is tapestries she weaves.

11 January

A letter from Bodil! That was completely unexpected, because the night train that carries the post was stuck in the snowy mountains again. Yes, Bodil is well now. That girl has mettle.

You build and build. Not on the mountain, not on sand, but in thin air somewhere in the future. Until you get to be so old that you realize none of it will become reality. Then you turn your gaze and your thoughts toward the past, and you build and build what could have been. Such is life.

The other day I bought a new phonograph, so now I have a nice stereo. So far I only have four records, and really only one that I like, Bach's *St. Matthew Passion,* played by the London Philharmonic, with Kathleen Ferrier as soloist. I play that record again and again. It was a gift from Bodil. I shall buy more records when I visit Bergen, really good records!

25 January

Received another record in the post! This time from Eileen B. Pettersen; she sends me Mozart. Beautiful, yes, what should I say?

The secret of Chinese poetry.

Time and again it strikes me: the Chinese didn't create their poems out of speculation. Instead, they wrote verses about the small and large events of their life. Just look at the titles in a selection by Wang Wei!

For Bodil Who Sent Me an LP of Bach and Handel

What would Wang Wei have done if you had
sent him an LP of Bach and Handel?
He would have played those sonatas again and again
in his hut by the Wang River in Chungnan
and dreamed himself away to his white clouds.
Then he would have made a poem and sent it to you.
That would have delighted not only you but posterity as well.
You, Bodil, will be the only one reading my poem.

28 January

Chinese Landscape - Note this: it is always a specific landscape being described, with place names, season, everything voiced precisely. Never do you find generalization that ends in moralizing!

These theoreticians, these ideologists! They are dangerous! Their theories are clever and seductive. Who can avoid getting caught in such beautiful traps?

3 February

While we are young, solitude can be a challenge, especially one's longing for women. But as you get to be older, you appreciate solitude more. You learn to savour it like an expensive wine. You gradually realize what a treasured thing it is! And precious! Solitude is the dearest of all luxuries. And the cheapest, like water and clean air. Still. While it lasts.

17 February

I wrote to Bodil. If she wants to move here, that's fine. I may be an old fool who doesn't have much to offer a lady like her, but I will provide food and a roof over her head. Should she find me impossible, she can always leave again. That's up to her. It can't end worse than that. She says she wants to come.

2 March

Today I called and spoke to Bodil. She was sitting there and waiting for me to call. It was good just to hear her voice, such a soft and warm voice.

It's new and unfamiliar for me to have a woman to think about, one whom I know is mine.

She says she will move in with me in the spring. We'll see how we get along. Certainly I have my doubts, but things might go better than I expect. Old habits are hard to change. I have been alone so long, that's all.

28 April

Today Bodil came to stay.

These days have been spent putting the house in order. There is much to straighten out or repair. A lot of work needs to be done before everything is in order. Bodil started weeding the flowerbeds around the house, which I guess hasn't been done since the war. Many of the perennials have died and will need to be replaced.

11 May 1976

A Poem Takes Form – Like a small flame that seizes upon dry grass, helplessly at first, flickering, searching for nourishment, then stronger, hissing, growing, consuming everything, raging into a storm, a force, a power to be reckoned with that consumes everything in her way.

5 January 1978

Went to the priest with a piece of paper; Bodil and I are planning to get married. And so it will happen at Voss, at the registrar's office, in three weeks. None too soon.

20 January

The River of Rhythm – Rhythm is a river.

You can push the boat out and float with the current, it will carry you.

Each new rhythm is a different river with its own rhythm. You need your own boat.

That's why you're safe with an established meter.

Writing poetry with free rhythms is fine and well, as long as the rhythms are there and carry you.

To write poetry without rhythm is like trying to sail on a dry riverbed.

27 January

Off to Voss and the Registrar's Office. Were married by Nygaard at one p.m. today. We got a piece of paper proving we were a duly married couple under Norwegian law. Well, better late than never.

Mountains No Longer Call Me

Mountains no longer call me.
I have lived long enough among cold glaciers.
I still make my way through the woods, listening
to the autumn wind, pausing by the tarns,
following the rivers. Even late in the year
you can find berries there.
To go further, you have to cross mountains.
Peaks stand there so you can get your bearings.

Emptying the Ash-Drawer

A few watchful stars hang above the mountains
when I step out. In the spring light, the pale snow-crust
gleams between the pine trunks.
Embers sizzle in the snow when I empty the ash-drawer.
Crumbling dreams scatter with the ashes in the grey wind.

Many Years of Practice with Bow and Arrow

That black dot in the
center, the bull's eye, that's what
you're supposed to hit – that's where
your arrow should stand quivering!
But that's not where the arrow goes.
You're close, closer and closer
– no, not close enough.
Then you have to go and fetch the arrows,
walk back, try again.
That black dot irks you.
Until you finally grasp
that where the arrow stands quivering
is also a center.

Two Rowboats on the Fjord

Two boats abreast on the fjord.
Fish on the thwart of both boats, and lines out.
The same fjord, sharing the same fine weather.
When one pulls a fish over the side
the other will wonder why
didn't that fish bite on my hook?
Such are their thoughts on this fine day.

New Tablecloth

New yellow cloth on the table.
And fresh white paper!
The words must come,
such fine cloth here
and such pristine paper!
There's new ice on the fjord
and birds have come to roost.

I'll Have to Think of Mischief

This joy is too much,
the kettle's about to boil over,
this scale-arm points skyward!
I'll have to think of mischief,
throw cold water on the kettle,
hang a stone on the scale,
fell the biggest pine I've got.

Up the River Valley

I step lightly on the stones
facing a cool gust off the river,
and I sing.
Grief is the source of strength,
glaciers weep in the sun.
Why do I walk easier
against than with?

Evening Service

The Evangelists hanging in chancel
hear their own words from the pulpit.
On the altar, candles flicker
in shadowy rings of doubt.
The congregation sings
to raise the roof.

Poppy

What elf came
to visit you last night?
Red silken garments
lie strewn about on the ground.
Are they his or yours
those black eyes?

Companion

You prefer
conversing with the wind,
having him as
your companion.

Or trees, plain,
well-poised and
wise trees.

But having me
as a companion?
It's good
you're used to
ghosts.

For Bodil Who Sent Me an LP of Bach and Handel

What would Wang Wei have done if you had
sent him an LP of Bach and Handel?
He would have played those sonatas again and again
in his hut by the Wang River in Chungnan
and dreamed himself away to his white clouds.
Then he would have made a poem and sent it to you.
That would have delighted not only you but posterity as well.
My poem, Bodil, will be read by you alone.

Carpet

Weave me a carpet, Bodil,
weave it of dreams and visions,
weave it of wind,
so that I, like a Bedouin, may
unroll it for prayer,
wrap it around myself
when I sleep,
and every morning call:
"The table is set!"
Weave it
as a cloak
against the cold,
a sail
for my boat!
One day I shall sit on that carpet
and sail away into
another world.

Sleep

Let us slip into
sleep, into
the calm dream,
slip in – two
lumps of dough into
the good oven
we call night.
And then waken
in the morning as
two golden
loaves!

The Rumbling River

Leaves come
debris comes
twigs and stumps –

I'll gladly carry it all
on my back
as long as I can,

when my strength fails,
I'll set it down, there
it will have to wait

until some other time.
I am most grateful
for streams and runoff,

they add to my strength.
If a wild tributary comes
dancing

she almost
takes my breath away,
we arch our backs

and wrestle and bustle.
Is she or I the one
who holds course?

Egil

If you lacked a shirt of armor,
you'd lash a flagstone to your chest;
if you lacked a sword,
you'd grab a cudgel.
I think you kept your wits
about you wherever you went.
But when you made poems,
you pulled that sheepskin
over your head.

By the Cabin of Einar Benediktsson

Low sun, high heavens, biting wind.
Wide, rock-strewn rowan woods
below misty mountains striped with snow.
Beyond, the ocean sends up pillars of white foam
around the steep crags.
A drystone wall creeps across the hills,
the barn has rotted away, the cabin remains.
Such is Herdisarvik on this December day.
I can feel the cold gust of his song.

Pausing Under a Lamppost on a Snowy Evening

(for the author Ernst Orvil on his eightieth birthday)

At last, I see it,
the solitary lamppost
at the crossroads

faithfully holding up
its umbrella of light
in the snowy evening.

I pause, even though I have
no love letter
asking

to be read. It just
seems strange
to pause here

under this umbrella of light
when it's snowing so,
I watch the flakes

float awhile
in that bright
ring of light

before they swirl
back into darkness or
or fall silently

And all around me in the darkness
it keeps snowing, snowing.

After Reading Guillevic

After reading
Guillevic
you are not
full,
but rather
a hungry, green
lupin in
river sand.

Paul Celan

Shut away in this spinning
ghost-house of life,
with peepholes,
each onto
their own reality
– that's how we live.
Most of us gather
by the largest hole,
telling ourselves:
"this is the world."

You sat alone
by your
peephole
– your eyes
black diamond,
your heart
a bloodstone.

The Big Scale

The old scale is
the most important thing
in the storage shed
(besides me, of course),
that's why it has its place
in the center of the floor;
there it ascertains
the weight of things
and the cost of shipping.
True enough, when I lift
a crate and heave a sack
I sense the weight,
but they have to go on the scale
– it has to have its say.
There's a bit of back and forth
between us as I add weights
to balance the load,
but more often than not
we agree – it tips, I nod:
"That's it!" – doesn't have to be right on the gram.
The scale is rusty, and my back is
stiff with arthritis
thankfully those weights are lighter
than the things I am weighing.
At times I notice people doubt
I'm being accurate.

People are odd.
When they're selling something
it should be heavy,
when they're shipping
it should be light.
The magistrate was in here the other day,
he too pondered the scale, no doubt
mindful of the things
he must weigh.
"This isn't a pharmacist's scale," I said,
but what I really had in mind was a scale
I saw at a goldsmith once;
he was weighing gold flakes
using tweezers.
I have often thought about
all the things a magistrate has to weigh:
right and wrong,
fines and punishments,
lives and fates.
Who adjusts
those weights,
that scale?

Night Express Running Late

Feel it
pick up speed,
feel it

surge forward
through the wind
– it'll catch up!

Careen through curves,
straighten, stretch
and stride

across bridges,
howl and haul
along its

furnace,
dive inside
the mountain.

Chug up the incline,
slow near the crest, rush
down the grade,

rods force wheels round
and round, clatter
against rails

Feel it
pick up speed,
feel it

surge forward
through the wind
it'll catch up!

The yellow crescent
moon is rushing
to keep up

through pine woods
on the hillside,
small stationmasters

with green flags
fade behind
like sticks

– no time
to stop, those
minutes are gone!

Carriage buffers
grind and bump, heads
thrown forward

in their seats,
glide into
dreams

suddenly snap out
when thoughts
sweep

beyond those lights
– what is

waiting for us?
No, let us
dream on

Feel it
pick up speed,
feel it

surge forward
through the wind
– it'll catch up!

When It Really Counts

Year in and year out you've bent your back over the books.
You have soaked up more knowledge
than you need for nine lives.
When it really counts, so little is needed
and your heart has always had this knowledge.

In Egypt the god of wisdom
had the head of an ape.

Mountains Are Hard To Move

Mountains are hard to move,
the oak root won't budge.
Who dares to tackle
the real problems of this world?
Bulls and elephants bear them on their backs
on long journeys, eagles rip out
bloody chunks and fly off
to cliffs and canyons,
wolves fight over them,
foxes circle the bait,
flies shit on them,
the magpie steals the silver,
the serpent wears the crown.

Ordinary Autumn Day, It's Snowing

It's dim in my den
    on a day like this.
        It occurs to me

this weather is
    great for sleds,
        people are

fetching firewood,
    the ground thaws

so neither young trees nor
    water pipes shall freeze
        – maybe I'm recalling

bumblebees and hedgehogs
    that now hide
        beneath the moss.

It's as if snowflakes
    race to reach
        the ground,

eager blind flecks
    burst forth in
        dizzying numbers

up there in the dusk
    – they swell, multiply
        swirl down

finally fall upward
   – no, the whole sky
      is falling
         again.

And the forecast
   promises more
      snow. And more

bombs in Vietnam.
   Greedily they drift
      over the poorest nations.

They talk and talk,
   words are
      snowing

over this world – imagine
   rice grains falling
      just as densely

over Biafra . . .
   I drift across
      the floor

and stand for a
   long time in front of
      my window.

Barometer

That golden arrow
I can move
as I please;
I prefer her
pointing to
good weather.

But I have
no dominion
over that
black arrow – mercilessly
she is under the sway
of cosmic forces
Reluctantly
I move
the golden one
accordingly.

I would prefer
to point her to
good weather
– hoping
the black one
will follow.

It's Time

Rockets
are pointed
and they land on the moon and Mars.
It's time
it's time
to sow our poison amongst the stars.

How Long Have You Slept?

This you dare,
to open your eyes
and look around?
Yes, you are here,
here in this world,
you are not dreaming,
it's just as you see it –
things here
are like this.
Like this?
Yes, thus and not otherwise.
How long have you slept?

Before Our Downfall

Christ's words
and the gruel of Heraclitus
can still save this world.
It's as simple as that.

On Svinøy Bridge

It's bracing to be crossing Svinøy Bridge on foot.
It soars above the harbor where boats
nudge each other and seagulls shout.
The smells of fish and oil and salty seas
fill my nose.

The clinkers' hammer blows resound from the cliff.
First they beached the trawler, MS *Vågakall,*
to be overhauled – then *Vågamøy*
and finally *Vågamot.*
They'll make a handsome trio
when they put to sea.

Snow in Castile

In Castile they greet the coming of snow
much as we welcome the flowering of apple trees in spring.
That's why Machado sings so sweetly of snow
– snow on Castile's rusty, sun-scorched hills!
A shadow sleeps beneath the snow on the olive branches.
I think of the orchards back home;
they're often damaged by frost.

Stare Miasto, Warsaw

Here you feel shameful.
From what people
devoid of will do you hail?
A people with a hundred years of liberty
who've barely managed to rebuild
a cathedral, let alone recall their tongue.

A proud people remembers its tyrants.
Sigismund Vasa is back
on his column in the Castle Square.

It was not to honor kings and bishops
they rebuilt this city, stone by stone,
but for all the unknown hands that slaved away
for them, and still found pleasure in the making.

Roads

Så ek å veg vega:
vegr var yfir
ok vegr undir
ok vegr å alla vega

I saw a road of roads,
a road under them
and a road over them
and a road on all sides.

Some went in circles,
others straight.

The fool sits
where he is seated.
The wise man walks
a part of each path.
Hell or heaven
awaits the man
who chooses
just one.

This they
told me of roads,
but not all.
Dreams reach
where feet cannot.
Some men have found
healing grass
on the isle of
their Loghica.

Orvar-Odd

Fine were the arrows you made,
better the ones you received from your father,
best were those the seer gave you.
You had the makings of an Arjuna,
the powers were for you as well as against you.

Many a wretch looms large
when he brags of your feats.
We know *one* legend rings true:
that the serpent sleeping in a man's pride
is often his undoing.

None shall be granted more room in our memory
than they are worth. I would have forgotten you
had you not found your way home to Ramsta.

To My Fingers

Oh, fingers
how often you are forced
to slave away for a cold brain
and a dead body!
If I refrained from writing
until you started whispering,
how good might my poems then be!
Then you might speak with tongues of fire!

I Pass the Arctic Circle

A man on the train points out the mountain cairn.
We're passing the Arctic Circle, he says.
At first we don't see any difference;
this land to the north looks the same,
but we know where we are headed.
I wouldn't have noticed this little event
if I hadn't the other day passed seventy.

We Thought This World Was Ours

We thought this world we see was made for us,
but what we believe shall not endure.
Surely there's a meaning to life – a wherefore?
No fool should try to answer when sages ask.

We do as he did: each of us forms his cross
and mistakes the road we are to walk;
we blame our nature for troubles and misfortunes,
instead of striving to escape our trap.

We curse life and the shortness of days,
shouting out the name of the man with the scythe.
But when the hour comes, we'll be counting every heartbeat

protesting that we're not ready to go.
Then we'll desire the bright fire of life!
We'll be at a loss and see what we have wasted.

Leaves Loosen

Let him have them,
    thinks the birch, and lets
        the wind carry off

her yellow leaves
    – she's left naked and
        cold in her thin twigs.

There's nothing like
    being poor, she
        has no other

place to stand
    than this
        bare crag.

The oak is also naked,
    but hardly poor.
        Wisely she sucks

strength from her leaves
    before letting them go,
        one by one.

It's long since she slept
    under grey bark,
        twisted branches

fumbling in the dark
    for stars, her roots
        sunk deep

in sheltered loam.

I Pause Beneath the Old Oak on a Rainy Day

It's not just the rain
that makes me pause
beneath the old oak
by the roadside. I feel
safe beneath that broad
crown, and it must be
old friendship that allows
the oak and me to stand there
silent, listening to raindrops
pattering against the leaves,
peering out at the grey day,
waiting, comprehending.
It occurs to us that the world is old
and both of us are aging.
Today I no longer stand dry,
the leaves have started to drop,
there's a sharp smell
in the raw air, I feel
the drops strike
through my hair.

Uncollected poems

Overleaf: Robert Bly was the first to render Hauge's voice into English – and before that Hauge translated Bly into Norwegian. The two poets enjoyed a correspondence over many years. Here we see them in the orchard on 17 April 1990, shortly before Olav H. Hauge died. (Archives of the Olav H. Hauge Centre, Ulvik, Norway.)

Excerpts from Hauge's Journals – through spring 1994

13 October 1980
Brought my woodworking bench into the living room. I'm going to glue the new tabletop, and it's best to have a bit of warmth for that. The gluing will take three days – it's a drop-leaf table with three sections. The tabletop will be solid oak, made from a tree my father felled and had milled into extra broad planks. That was during the war, so those planks ought to be nice and dry by now. They'll make a good solid tabletop that should withstand rough treatment and being pounded by a fist.

15 October
Went to Storlidi for peat moss, in which we store carrots for the winter. Even though temperatures dropped below freezing last night, we gathered three sacks, enough for Pål and Kari as well. Øian at Boklaget called to say that my book has been printed. He'll put a couple in the mail today.

Well, *Collected Poems* is also being released in a new edition, with corrections and a batch of recent poems I've called *Gleanings.*

22 October
Finished my table. Good, solid oak makes a beautiful tabletop. Things are looking up in the house now; we've gotten a lot done this year. First the great new annex, which is a fine investment, then repairs on the chimneys, new firewalls, new gutters on the whole house, various and sundry furniture, and I have to mention our modernization of the kitchen last summer – all in all, a great expense.

20 May 1982
To only listen to your own voice, your own demands, your own feelings, that's daring for a poet. He may be considered an eccentric, a hermit.

War. The Falkland Islands. Who starts something like that? A handful of politicians who cynically sacrifice the lives of young men for power. If these men's duty compelled them to wager their own lives instead, perhaps they would have thought twice. In this way the kings of old were more honest, being in the forefront of the battle.

We're painting the house. Long ladders are quite a struggle (by the way, we were able to borrow steel ladders that can be joined). Scraping, applying putty and painting. A young man is giving us a hand; otherwise the effort is mine and Bodil's.

We don't have so much time in this world, but we carry on as though we expect eternal life. In that regard, that snail has progressed further.

It is when you are most burdened by duties that your desire to write and make poetry is at its strongest.

Most philosophers resemble the inchworm. He knows his leaf, but when he reaches the edge, he stands there waving his head in the air.

The young soldier who had to die on those desolate islands in the South Atlantic also had a right to live.

I have read a lot of theory without learning anything. I hope that I'm able to discard it as quickly as water off a duck's back.

7 July

First Comes the Word – People complain that our young people are succumbing to drugs. Who has led them astray, lured them to experiment with all these substances? Wasn't it the wise, the prophets? Think of the 1960s. How many world-famous authors and scientists advised people to try mescaline, cannabis, and LSD? Aldous Huxley, S. Clay Wilson, Jack Kerouac, Allen Ginsberg – oh, it is a long list. We might also mention R.D. Laing, Timothy Leary, and Henri Michaux. The psychedelic experience was supposed to be the answer. In a simple, straightforward way. A single pill would open the Gates of Paradise. Unfortunately, all too often it was the Gates of Hell that opened.

Around 10 July

Nietzsche's "Umwertung" is actually rather vulgar and simple-minded. It's so easy to turn concepts and values topsy-turvy, changing a few pluses to minuses. Releasing Barabbas and making him into a hero seems so simple.

Many who write about Nietzsche say that he cannot be accused of harbouring a Nazi ideology. They can't know his last writings. You cannot find more raw thoughts about power and politics in print. Most of those who read him consider these to be the ravings of a madman, and so they are.

No, I believe Nietzsche bears much responsibility for the fascist movements; in his books you find the main tenets of their teachings. No excuses should be made.

Then they continue in the usual manner, claiming that he represents the future, that he is the harbinger of something new. Nothing could be further from the truth. Nietzsche is reactionary, and the ideals he proclaims have, unfortunately, held sway in this world for the last thousand years. Both in aesthetics and politics the world is ruled by aristocrats. All in all, Nietzsche's philosophy is a defense of the old.

30 August

Suspicious – Shaman. Some try to be one, but are they real? Robert Bly has taken on a tone and manner reminiscent of a shaman. I read of Sereptie, a Siberian Samoyed shaman whose story is told by Waldemar Bogoras. Then I though of Bly's book of poetry, *Sleepers Joining Hands.* The shaman himself tells of his experiences, and there is something in his tone and presentation that reminds me of that poem. The theme is initiation into the life of the shaman, into the role of the seer.

Perhaps that is no coincidence; perhaps Bly is a shaman.

10 September

Rain. The plums are bursting. Reread Ellis' essay "The Art of Writing." I still think he is good. As I do Santayana. That's to be expected; his name is renowned!

An unexpected package from the U.S.A. Robert Bly has sent me four books. One book about himself, his large anthology of nature poems, and two others. He carries on, does readings and gives speeches, translates, writes, and makes poetry. I see that he has translated three of my poems in *Ploughshares,* which he enclosed.

13 November

Why? – Why isn't Po Chü-Yi as widely known and translated as Li Po? You might well ask. I suppose it's because he didn't write much about wine and women and metaphysical matters. In Europe, we have long believed that is what a poet must do in order to be considered a great poet. Writing about injustices and everyday matters won't do.

8 January 1983
It snowed last night. And snow flurries today. Yet it's still mild – only one degree below freezing. Yes, there's more than a trifle snow today, the snowplows have their work cut out for them. This evening there are blue gaps between the clouds, a few stars, and it's colder.

Leafing through old papers is like raking up old leaves. You might find the occasional larva, perhaps a cocoon – and you never know what butterfly might emerge from that.

11 January

Haiku or Tanka?

Three lines are too few.
You need five.
Then you have room
For everything:
Life, grief and death.

5 February
You Must Walk – Sitting down to write poetry is no use; this is ancient wisdom. Bjørnson would pace to and fro when he was writing. And Olav Vinje praised mountain hikes as a way of getting good ideas. According to his wife, Mandelstam would always be walking when he worked on a poem. The Greek philosophers walked ideas as they were thinking, we know. "How many shoes did Dante wear out writing the *Divina Comedia*?" asks Mandelstam.

"Poetry is the yeast of the world, a sweet-voiced labor," says Mandelstam. Mrs. Mandelstam's book, *Hope Against Hope,* fills me with desire to make poems again, despite my age.

2 April
The weather is unchanged. Bodil left for Oslo today; she plans to be back Sunday evening. I have much to do. I have to prepare potatoes for planting, setting them aside to sprout. Then I intend to put up more shelves; my li-

brary keeps growing and I don't know what to do with all the books. I have again been concentrating on the Chinese authors, especially those of the Sung Era. Su Tung-Po is an excellent poet. And there are so many others! They never tire of describing nature and the landscape, seen in all kinds of seasons and weather. Oh, those long rivers, with their birds and boats, but first and foremost the stars!

The starlings have arrived.

5 January 1985

Where Is the Landscape? – Where can the landscape be seen in poetry? Nature? The seasons? The weather? The ocean, mountains and forests? The flowers? The grass? The trees. There is no longer any mention of species. At most there are trees, flowers, grass, a bird ... that is the reach of our knowledge. A Norwegian painter or so-called poet doesn't know the difference between hazel and rowan, elm and ash, that's for sure.

No, the portrayal of nature is a forgotten art. Consider Wilhelm Ekelund, for example. Look at his wonderful depictions of the landscape. He follows the seasons in all their subtleties, the passage of days, morning and evening, sun and shadow. He knew the trees, the plants.

Easter Sunday 1986

Wrote the last poem for the children's book Bodil and I are making together. She is making illustrations and I have made some poems – one poem for each of our twenty-nine letters, from A to Å.

29 June

Sunday. Sunny and warm. Bly called from Utne, and by eleven a.m. he was here. His wife had continued on to Bergen. It was a short visit, because at one p.m. he had to meet his wife in Kvanndal. So we all got in the car and drove him to Kvanndal and Utne.

"A great man on the road," was the caption on a photo of Bly taken by Jan Erik Vold, published in *Basar*. And that's true. Robert Bly is a large fellow who looms high wherever he is. A great man, both physically and intellectually.

Kabir is a man to Bly's liking. Jacob Boehme is another. That says a lot about the man, more than my description of him does. This time he spoke of Thoreau; Bly is editing a selection of his poems. He talked a bit about Emerson as well.

8 July

Bly encourages us to examine the poets of old in order to learn from their mistakes. Practical leaning, you might say, and very American, but I hardly think that's the reason he himself reads those poets. I think he is looking for healing water, spiritual nourishment.

Bly, however, has made Pope's words his personal slogan: "The life of a writer is a warfare upon earth." He seems a happy warrior.

9 July

Cutting hay, chopping wood, cooking food. Pacing to and from in the yard. Looking at the weather, contemplating, reading a bit during my breaks. Thus I pass the day. The weather answers with a shower, then sunlight breaking through the clouds.

1 August 1987

I will never do this again. Bodil showed me how to start the car, accelerate, steer, and brake. Well, it went fine here in the yard. Then we drove up to the meadow. She turned the car around and I was supposed to drive it back down. Most of the way it rolled on its own; I only had to steer. But as we turned into the yard and I had to accelerate, I sped up bit too much and the car flew into the corner of the house. The right headlight is shattered, and the bumper and the side of the car are damaged. I hit my knee against the edge of the dashboard. Bodil, who was sitting beside me, is uninjured. We sat there stunned, shocked at my stupidity. The corner of the house was badly damaged as well. The car was still running, though. Bodil telephoned the company that sold it to her, and they told her to bring it in for repairs. The next day she drove it to Voss. I swore that I would never drive a car again. I'm limping a bit, but it doesn't seem like my knee is badly injured. It put a jolt in us. A car is a dangerous means of transport!

2 November 1988

Another Nobel Prize Winner – In 1935, the Portuguese neurologist Antonio Moniz came up with the idea of cerebral surgery to cure people of mental illness. In 1949 they gave him the Nobel Prize in Medicine for his wonderful invention. He called it *lobotomy.* That's a weighty word. A word that commanded respect. Pity those who fell victim to the surgeons' scalpels. The most defenseless were first in line. The Pope condemned these surgeries, and the Russians never allowed them. How many patients throughout the world were destroyed? Those were dark years for anyone threatened with being committed to an asylum, I know that much.

Around the same time Moniz was carrying out his surgeries, an Italian psychiatrist was experimenting with giving his mental patients electroshock treatments. It was terrorization under the name of treatment. Supposedly neither of these two treatments are used much today. I wouldn't be too sure of that.

18 August 1989

Today I am eighty-one years old. They used to say that was an advanced age. True, aging doesn't arrive alone, as most people will find if they get old.

2 December

Bright. It's going to be sunny today, the 2nd.

"In literature it is only the wild that attracts us. Dullness is but another name for tameness. It is the uncivilized free and wild thinking in *Hamlet* and in the *Iliad,* in all the scriptures and mythologies, not learned in the schools, that delights us. As the wild duck is more swift and beautiful than the tame, so is the wild – the mallard – thought, which 'mid falling dews wings its way above the fens. A truly good book is something as natural, and as unexpectedly and unaccountably fair and perfect, as a wildflower discovered on the prairies of the West or in the jungles of the East."

–Thoreau (from *Walking*)

15 February 1992

Dagfinn Tveito came to present an idea recently: a book about Ulvik village and me. But I fear such a venture will cause much discord. I have always been unsocial and stood apart from the life of the village. It was particularly bad in my youth; I spent my entire youth as a hermit. That marks a man. I think I'll decline the idea of a book whose main character is me.

Foul Weather – The other evening, I walked up to the high pasture at Rossvoll. On a hunch I headed to Anfinnsgården farm, intending to go by way of their farmyard. Yes, as I walked the new road below Løypet, I reached a gate that was securely closed. I untied it and secured it again after passing through, and with good intentions I headed toward the farm. The old apple trees were still there, which my father planted seventy-five years ago, the oldest on the farm.

Suddenly I was confronted by Stein Olav's ram! I had forgotten that he grazed freely there every summer; if only I had remembered. He walked toward me, coolly and deliberately. I tried to talk him calm, to scratch him gently. But, no, he just nodded and was dead set on butting me! I did my best to deter him with my fists, but that didn't faze him in the least. What was I to do? Take off my shoe? No, so I kicked him right in the forehead. He didn't even blink, but kept lunging at me. I threw myself against him, trying to wrestle him to the ground. Although it was a steep incline, he kept his footing, sturdy as a rock. Above us stood the old apple tree. I bent down a branch and tried to break it off. It hung there, half-broken, right in front of the ram. That was my salvation – immediately he started eating apple leaves, his favorite meal, and forgot all about me. I ran down the hill, jumped over the fence to safety. I'm sure my blood pressure must have hit three-hundred, and my heart pounded fiercely in my chest. I had to sit down by the overhanging rock until I calmed down. As I walked toward the farmyard, the ram came after me again, braying and ready for a new fight. I didn't sleep that night.

23 August 1993

What would I have amounted to if I hadn't read some Schopenhauer in my youth? A pig-headed positivist? Bereft of Schopenhauer's flute music?

24 January 1994

Snow. Almost three feet deep on the meadow here at Rossvoll. Great conditions for skiing! But I am lying here like a hibernating bear, as they used to say. I haven't been outside at all, feeling rather feeble this winter.

17 April

Great things have happened here. Happened? No, but some rather unusual people have been to visit, causing quite an upheaval in our quiet existence. Robert Bly came and stayed two days with us. And he spent a day at Bleie visiting relatives. On his last evening, there was a celebration for him at Hardanger Folk Museum in Utne. He read some of his poems and Bodil read my translations. A man from the American Institute in Oslo made a speech, and afterwards there was a dinner for Bly. Professor Idar Stegane was toastmaster. Afterwards, Arvid Torgeir Lie came back to Ulvik with us and spent the night. Bly is considering translating some of his poems.

The days Bly spent here exhausted me.

16 May 1994

Yesterday, the 15th of May, Jan Erik Vold and Tøger came from Hallingskeid, accompanied by Jan Erik's oldest son who is fourteen years old. Nineteen years ago, Jan Erik and Tøger visited me, coming the same route from Osete. Jan Erik complained that the route seemed steeper and more strenuous now. Tøger, who is almost six foot seven, is in better shape. They arrived at six in the evening, calling from Osa; Bodil drove to pick them up. They were famished and ate hearty portions of rib of lamb. There was snow until Osete. At this time of year, the descent can be quite challenging, rather icy and stony. Few use that route now; people prefer to descend by way of Viermyr.

They stayed with us until Sunday. Tøger helped Bodil plant potatoes, before they headed for Voss and took the afternoon train home to Oslo.

The day was sunny and radiant.

Each Time a Poem Glows

Each time I sense the poem in me glow
I know this is the sound of song to sing.
O, shall not I receive the fiery seed
to rhyme and let the wave of music flow?
This spring day fills me with such sacred cheer
that golden blossoms open – do you hear
the larches sound their exultation?
But fairest I sing from bleeding heart.

(*from Journals, 1928*)

Imaginative Man

Man is strange!
Place him on a rock
in the sea,
and he will transform it
into a garden;
lock him away
and he will make
his prison into a castle
– or even steer the madhouse
into the starry sky,
night after night.
Place him on a lonely planet
in space,
and he will fill
the heavens with gods,
the mountain with trolls,
place dwarves in the crag
and elves in the woods,
phantoms at sea,
sprites in the falls
– weather spirits, wind spirits,
night-elves and water spirits.

And when he thinks
it too dreary to die,
he finds another way:
He imagines life
after death, joyous
realms and kingdoms,
Paradise, Asgard,
Hades and Hel.

(1947)

Fence

"It's best to keep what's yours separate," said Torstein,
and fenced himself in behind the barb wire he stretched
through the hills and down to the shore.
Thus he safeguarded his farm.

The farmers of old would send their sheep to pasture,
together, but many things have changed.
Torstein lies in the cemetery now, his grave
framed by white cement.

(*1947*)

To Knotgrass (*Sclerantus*)

You're so small no one sees you,
thoughtlessly they tread on you.
Truth be told, you act so humble,
scarcely drawing attention,
yet for someone surely you shine
huddled there by your grey rock.

(*from Journals, July 1953*)

Have You Seen the Ocean?

Have you seen the ocean tug driftwood,
tin cans and tables
on its rolling swells,
how carelessly it sways
and carries it all
– lifts it on its wave crests,
shows forth,
turns, lets shine,
then embraces it again
and lifts it once more,
always playful,
always carelessly tossing it
– this is just rubbish to me,
toys; nothing
about this moves these lips
to smile?

(1948)

A Westland River

Clutching a cliff
by the misty falls
ferns gather dew,
the river dances forth
cool and wild,
races foamy white
over black boulders
and through empty weirs,
green-sheathed she toils
through deep dark pools,
then bright as a glacier spreads
by islets and sandy banks,
angry swirls tug
at fishing lines,
fence posts march
into the water
and are gone –

(from Journals, July 1953)

Why Shouldn't

Why shouldn't the stars and sun shine,
why shouldn't the snowy peaks rise,
why shouldn't ocean and forests sing,
why shouldn't waterfalls tumble
and eagles soar above the abyss?
The day is huge, but night is larger still,
for that's where dreams grow.
That's where the boat is built
that shall carry you over the Great Sea
and the bridge that leads you
across the abyss,
and that's where
wings are made,
if you choose.

(1960)

They Rule

They sit on the county council.
And they haven't even
read Plato.

(1966)

There Are Legends

There are legends about Earth.
She is renowned.

And many come here
to rest,
to drink
and quench their thirst,
eat their fill,
to meet woman
and
man.

Here are grassy fields,
sandy shores, rivers,
forests, seas –

It all depends.
But it's not safe here.

(1969)

Why Don't You Try It Yourself

These small poems
can't have
cost you much?

A few scraps of paper
and some ink
– surely those little words come
of their own accord?

Why don't you
try it yourself
– make a poem?
You don't understand
how a poem
can astonish
the girls.

You can trim
hair and beard
any way you please,
but those words
will be read
with a smile.

(*1969*)

Thoughts From a Two-Day Journey

Voss

I won't say anything
about Voss; the locals
have plenty to say about it themselves.

Kjosfossen

This is the famous waterfall.
Unfortunately there is no water
in it now.

Flåm

The river shines brightly in Flåm.
Bright are the poems of Per Sivle as well;
like the river they flow
from deep springs.

Aurland

Rowans with red berries
on the meadows of Aurland,
familiar and cherished.

Lærdal

Before, Lærdal was
only wind, crofters
and tamarisk.
Now birches and nettles
also flourish.

On board MS Skagastøl
Tame gulls,
grouchy tourists.
Skagastøl is carrying
quite a load.

Borgund stave church
Had the salmon swum farther
than Sjursteigfossen Falls,
old Borgund church would not stand here.

Hemsedal
Yet another village that
keeps its head down. I
think I see why.

Gol
The old stave church stands
at an outdoor museum in Oslo.
Here at home are supermarkets and kiosks
that sell porn mags.

At Dyranut
The farm they came from is abandoned.
Here their heirs are arguing
about plots on which to build
cafés.

Eidfjord

We need to build a new church
for our priest!
Keep the old one for tourists
to gawk at.

Bashō

You've said so much and sung
about so much more, but I
have been
gone only two days.

Your legs were thin,
your song was soft.
So light your satchel
and your mind like
a meandering wind.

(*from Journals,* 1972)

That One Word

This is what I wanted
to say to her.
That one word.
But it has to be
just a hint,
a trace,
a riddle,
a dream
– it must come
like a wing
at night –
come as the wind
with eyes
of oceans and stars.

(1974)

Issa Thought –

If I am good,
I can expect to live
many lives,
but this one
I shall use
for poetry.

(1979)

The Cell

I belonged here.
Perhaps I always
longed for here.
A naked cell.
Worn floorboards,
a heavy oak door
with a small slot.
In one corner a mattress
some woolen blankets,
a rubber bedpan,
that's all.
Below the window
a radiator
encased in steel;
such a wondrous sound
when I beat it
and sang.
Strange marks on the wall
and letters scratched in stone.
Iron bars on the window,
but each day the sun came
and laid a golden slab
on the floor.
Here as well.

Set Not My Ashes

Set not my ashes
in a cold grave.
Spread them on the wind,
cast them into the sea!

Long was I trapped
in pain and sorrow.
Heart, release now
your tears of grief.

My soul, cool
your longing fire,
sway in a wildflower
on a foreign shore!

A pensive poet with his books, 1991. Olav H. Hauge was very conscious of his linguistic heritage, insisting on using many old words and phrases from his native Ulvik – foreign readers aren't the only ones who have to reach for a dictionary!
Idar Stegane, Hauge expert and decades-long friend of the poet, and Professor of Nordic Literature and Languages, believes that the authentic dialects of Western Norway, especially those of the remote valleys and inner fjords – such as Hauge's Ulvik dialect – may have been closer to the spoken Old Norse than modern Icelandic is.
Photo: Odd Nerbø. (Archives of the Olav H. Hauge Centre, Ulvik, Norway.)

Notes on the Poems

Embers In the Ashes (1946)

"Foxgloves In the Gravel Pit" – This early poem, describing how plants gradually reclaim an abandoned gravel pit, is clear evidence of Hauge's deep understanding of ecological balance and the natural processes that unfold over long time spans.

"Prayer" and "Always I Expect to Find" are included in *Norsk salmebok* – the hymn book used by the Norwegian Church. Four lines from "Prayer" are carved into Olav H. Hauge's tombstone in Ulvik:

> Open my eyes, Oh Lord,
> that I better may gaze
> upon your marvel, not only
> its outward glaze.

Beneath the Crag (1951)

"Shaking the Snow Off Young Trees" – Apple trees and orchard tasks are recurring themes in Hauge's poems.

"Beneath the Crag" – The key word in the Norwegian title *Under bergfallet* means rock outcrop, crag, or overhanging cliff, particularly the potential rockslides from these. For many farms in Western Norway, nearby crags and cliffs pose an ever-present danger.

"This Is Your Burden" – This poem refers to Volund, an elf and master smith who is the hero of the *Volund Saga of the Poetic Edda*. Imprisoned by a Swedish king, and hamstrung so he could not flee, Volund escaped by making wings! In Hauge's poem, it is Volund's Achilles tendons that are severed. Volund's saga parallels the Greek legend of Daedalus from Greek mythology.

"The Back-Cracking Hug" – *Ryggjakneppa* is a traditional trial of strength. Two combatants, embracing each other in "a back-cracking hug," try to throw their opponent to the ground.

"Tongue and Bell" – This poem, one of the final ones in this 1951 collection, is perhaps Hauge's first "thing-poem." These played a key role in getting the younger Norwegian poets that formed a clique around *Profil* literary magazine to celebrate Olav H. Hauge as one of their own. Another noteworthy early poem of this type is "The Axehead," in Hauge's next collection.

Slowly the Woods Redden in the Gorge (1956)

"Do the Next Man a Favor" – The hamlet of Osa is situated at the head of the Osafjord, an arm of the Hardangerfjord. Before World War II there was no road along the fjord, and the only way to get to Osa was by boat, or by an onerous trail across the mountains. Ødvinstø is a smaller hamlet a few miles farther out in the fjord.

"The Snowfield" – Hauge's poem is entitled *Bumannen*, the name of this snowfield, i.e., a patch of snow or tiny glacier on the shaded side of Mount Onen. It may grow or shrink with the weather and seasons, but never entirely disappears – always visible from the poet's farm. From below, the snowfield appears to have the profile of a man, hence the Norwegian name *Bumannen*.

The "Seventh Master of the House" refers to a well-known Norwegian fairytale. A young wanderer stops at a blacksmith and asks for shelter for the night. He is referred to his father, who in turn refers him to his father... It turns out that seven generations are living in the same house! Finally the wanderer meets the "seventh master," a shriveled-up old man hanging in a horn on the wall. Some interpret the story, one of many fairytales collected by Peter Christen Asbjørnsen and Jørgen Moe, as a sly commentary on bureaucracy. It was made into a film by Ivo Caprino.

"The Axehead" – This is another of the first "object poems" that made Norway's young modernists applaud Hauge as one of their own.

"Korea" – One of Olav H. Hauge's few overtly political poems.

"The Golden Cock" – In the second line, Hauge writes *Miklagard,* the old Norse name for Constantinople or Byzantium.

On the Eagle's Perch (1961)

"Let Your Grief Go" --In Norse mythology, Gjoll is the river that separates the underworld from the world of the living.

"Steel Coil" – The steel coil described in this poem is the coil spring in a door lock.

"An Old-Fashioned Norwegian" – The author referred to in the final stanza is Hans Ernst Kink (1865–1926).

"The Meadow at Kvannskorane" – Kvannskorane is a meadow high up the mountainside, about three miles from Ulvik. The grass growing in this distant outfield was dried on hay-wires and used for winter fodder on the farms at Hakestad.

"The Message Stick" – From Viking times up until the early 1900s, when a council was summoned or there was other important news, a message stick was sent from farm to farm, some of them quite isolated. Message sticks were often hollow wooden tubes, wherein was the written message.

"Kuppern on Skates in Squaw Valley" – At the 1960 Olympics in Squaw Valley, California, the Norwegian speed skater Knut "Kuppern" Johannessen set a new world record of 15:46.6 for the 10,000-meter, shaving forty-six seconds off the previous record.

"The Blue Land" – *Yggdrasil,* referred to in the final line of this poem, is an immense ash that embraces all of the nine worlds mentioned in Norse mythology. Its three roots extend into *Niflheim* (the underworld), *Jotunheim* (land of the giants) and *Asgard* (home of the gods). *Yggdrasil* is mentioned in both the elder *Poetic Edda,* and the younger *Prose Edda* written by Snorri Sturluson in the 13th century.

"This Is Not the Kingdom of the Poor" – This poem refers to Valen Psychiatric Hospital, the asylum where Hauge was a patient for long periods of his life.

"To a Painting by Nikolai Astrup" – The Norwegian painter Nikolai Astrup (1880–1928) lived most of his life on the farm in Jølster where he grew up. The painting referred in the poem is *Spring Night In the Garden,* a subject that Astrup painted numerous times. Astrup was a master colorist and his landscapes are highly treasured.

"The Wheat Field" – The print in question hung on the wall in of Ward D, a closed section of Valen Psychiatric Hospital, where Hauge spent a considerable amount of time.

The reader may be struck by the contrast between the dreamy tranquility of the wheat field in Hauge's poem and the turbulence of van Gogh's last painting, *Wheatfield with Crows.* While Hauge wrote his poem based on a recollection, Vincent executed his painting while under the care of Dr. Paul Gachet, shortly after leaving an asylum in Saint-Rémy.

Droplets On the Eastern Wind (1966)

"There Is Nothing Scary" – The word *tussalusi* in the third line means woodlouse, but may also refer to certain underground female spirits.

"Leiv Eiriksson" – This poem, of course, refers to the Viking explorer (ca 970–102) who sailed to Vinland, establishing a settlement in Newfoundland. Like Hauge, I have used the Norwegian spelling of his name.

"Sveigdir" was a mythical Swedish king. According to the *Ynglinga Saga,* written by Snorri Sturluson approx 1225, Sveigdir was lured by a dwarf into a mountain, never to reappear.

"Ogmund Rides Home" – The crusader Ogmund, who hailed from a farm in Hauge's home district, is briefly mentioned in *The Saga of Haakon Haakonsson.* In 1217 he joined a crusade to the Holy Land, taking a circuitous route to Jerusalem, sailing northward past the North Cape and down the rivers through Russia.

Spånheim (also written Sponheim) lies across the mountains, on the road to Voss.

Mount Vassfjøro (1633 m) is a mountain near Ulvik. Often veiled in fog, or snow and ice, it is reminiscent of the white hoods traditionally worn by women in Hardanger, which are now part of the Hardanger variant of the national costume. The mountain is a prominent part of the view from Hauge's farm.

"In Memory of Old Vamråk" – Old Vamråk was one of Hauge's fellow patients at Valen Psychiatric Hospital.

"The Hay Wire" – During the hay-drying season, wires were suspended between poles, at various levels, and grass was cut with a scythe and hung on the wires to dry. The hay provided winter fodder for a farm's livestock and horses.

Today this is a rarer sight, as the hay more and more often is harvested mechanically and gathered into large, plastic-covered balls, in which the hay ferments and is preserved.

"The Estuary" – In a deep lake, even when thick ice covers the surface, the bottom layers of water maintain a constant 4°C (39.2°F). Thus when water was drawn from the lake depths, as in the pipe tunnel project Hauge describes in the poem, the warmer water kept the cove or bay of the fjord open.

"Mountain Farm" – Støl is a mountain farm or rather an outfarm, i.e., a summer pasturage often shared by several farms, with simple shelters for the shepherds and livestock, and other building that might be needed. In Scotland this is referred to as a *shieling*.

"Acestes" – The story of Acestes is told in Virgil's *Aenid*, verse 485–544.

"Bertolt Brecht" – Bertolt Brecht (1898–1956), German poet and playwright. Hauge translated twenty-five poems by Brecht.

"The Watcher" – A flexible branch onto which the fishing line is attached when ice fishing. Movement of "the watcher" indicates a strike or catch.

"Old Poet Tries His Hand as a Modernist" – Hauge was bemused by the young modernist poets who embraced only parts of his lyrical productions, such as his object poems. Throughout his entire literary life he also wrote rhymed poems and sonnets, as well as making acclaimed translations of structured poems.

"I Have Three Poems" – The Emily referred to is, of course, Emily Dickinson. Hauge translated a number of her poems.

"Autumn" – A scimitar is a curved sword that was favored in numerous Middle Eastern countries.

"In My Father's House" – The Odin referred to in the poem is not the Norse god, but one of the main characters in *The People of Juvik,* a six-volume novel cycle by Olav Duun (1876–1939). Odin's boat is overtaken by a storm and capsizes when he is rowing a girl across the fjord, but they survive. Later Odin drowns during a second boating accident.

A Village Romeo and Juliet is an opera by English composer Frederick Delius, first performed in 1907. It is based on a short story by Swiss author Gottfried Keller.

"Stettarbekken" – Usually Stettarbekken creek is modest, indeed, but after a heavy rainfall it is very visible as you enter the road to Hauge's farm.

"It Is That Dream" – Without doubt this is Hauge's most quoted poem. It is often recited at funerals.

"T'ao Ch'ien" (365–427 C.E.), 陶潛, also known as Tao Qian or Tao Yuanming, was a great poet of the Jin Dynasty. Although he was considered reclusive, his imagery is more often that of the garden and countryside than the wilderness. The poet often wrote of his deep appreciation of wine. In his poem, Hauge speaks of serving him a glass of Hardanger's legendary apple cider!

"The Salmon Weir" – This traditional salmon trap was built of logs, allowing the salmon to swim in but not out. No longer in use, salmon weirs were used to catch salmon in many of the rivers of Western Norway.

"The Cropped Hazel" – Technically, the reference is to a *pollarded* hazel (cut off at man-height), as opposed to one that is *coppiced* (cut off at ground level, fostering many new shoots). On the farms of Western Norway, trees – most typically ash, birch, rowan, elm or linden – were often pollarded so that their leaves could more easily be reached and harvested for winter fodder.

"The Big Apple Tree Outside My Window" – In recent decades, the selection of apples in Norwegian supermarkets has been standardized, and the number of varieties greatly reduced, just as it has in other countries. When the Farmers Cooperative (*Gartnerhallen*) stopped accepting the apples from his large tree, Hauge cut it down to improve the view.

Today the great apple trees of Hardanger are few and far between. Instead the orchards are comprised of what are called "bush" apples in the trade, meaning the varieties are grafted onto dwarf or semi-dwarf rootstocks, with the trees planted very close together and pruned to around man-height. This intensive practice, where the apples can be reached for pruning, spraying and picking without the use of ladders, as though they were grapevines, has largely replaced the traditional orchard model of twenty-five- to thirty-foot trees planted every twenty or so feet apart, because it bears younger and more productively and offers better control of pests.

"The Trapping Pit" – When you fly over Norway, you might easily conclude that the inhabitants have left their mark on only a tiny fraction of the landscape. However, as you wander on foot, you will see mile upon mile of drystone walls dividing the landscape, foundations of old houses and, if you know where to look, also Viking grave mounds and ancient trapping pits. Hauge was intimately familiar with the surrounding landscape and its history.

"William Blake" – Hauge had a life-long fascination with William Blake (1757–1827), of whom he translated a number of poems into Norwegian.

"Gérard de Nerval" – A number of French poets were greatly esteemed by Hauge, including Gérard Labrunie – who is far better known by his penname Gérard de Nerval (1808–55). Like Hauge, Nerval was an avid translator, rendering Goethe's *Faust*, and poems by Heinrich Heine and others into French.

"Read Lu Chi and Write a Poem" – Lu Chi (251–303 C.E.), 陸機, also written Lu Ji or referred to as Shiheng, was a poet of the Three Kingdoms period. In addition to poetry, Lu Chi wrote literary criticism that became highly influential. Lu Chi was killed after falsely being accused of treason.

"Sogn" – Sogn is a district in Sogn og Fjordane county, several mountain ranges and one fjord north of Hauge's Ulvik.

Skjær is a farmstead in Sogn.

King Bele or Beli was the chieftain of Balestrand mentioned in *Fridtjov's Saga*

The Eggjum Stone, discovered on Eggja Farm in Sogndal, is covered with two-hundred runes. Scholars are still arguing about precisely how to interpret the 7th-century inscription.

The poem's last stanza refers to a bronze statue of the legendary hero Fridtjov, bequeathed to Sogn by Kaiser Wilhelm II. The statue, thirty-four feet tall and on a thirty-nine foot tall base, that stands in the village of Vangsnes. Not all locals have been equally grateful for the – shall we say – prominent gift of the German Emperor, who was quite the Norwegophile…

For instance in January of 1904, when the Kaiser received news that a tragic fire had reduced much of Ålesund to ashes, he immediately ordered four ships to sail north. Loaded with food and medicine, blankets and building materials, his aid arrived before any help from Oslo did. Also, when World War I broke out, Kaiser Wilhelm II was on holiday in the village of Balestrand, visiting a painter friend. Norwegian authorities gave the Kaiser the ultimatum to leave Norwegian territory by six p.m. that very day. Not being a man to have his pleasures cut short, Kaiser Wilhelm took his jolly good time drinking his tea, enjoying conversation with his host, and savoring impressions of the surrounding landscape – before heading full steam out the fjord aboard his yacht, minutes before the deadline expired!

"Looking at the Postmark on Your First Letter" – In this poem Hauge refers to Greek mythology. Até (also spelled Atë) is the goddess of mischief, folly and delusion. She often brings about the ruin of a hero for his hubris. The Erinyes, also known as the Furies, are goddesses of the underworld who are sworn to vengeance.

"Christmas Sheaf" – In Scandinavia, wheat or other grain is tied into a bundle (sheaf) and hung outside, thus sharing the bounty of the harvest with the birds that do not migrate south in the winter.

"Dance" – The key word in this poem is almost impossible to translate. Hauge's title and refrain, *ir,* means restlessness and anxiety, shift and change —as in the forever shifting and changing dance of Creation. The fidgeting of the Universe, if you will.

In this poem, Olai is a farmer or manual laborer who happens to be digging a ditch.

"*Dieu de la Danse*" – Vaslav Nijinsky (1889–1950) was perhaps the greatest 20th-century male dancer – and a tragic figure. He spent much of the last thirty years of his life in insane asylums.

"Arctic Mother 1944" – Hauge's poem, inspired by an etching by Kaare Espolin Johnson (1907–1944), casts a harsh light on the destruction of Finnmark during World War II. The German army, retreating from the Russian forces liberating the northernmost part of Norway, carried out a scorched-earth strategy.

Gleanings (1980)

Gleanings (*Janglestrå*) is a section of new poems that Hauge added to a new edition of his *Collected Poems* in 1980. This book-length section contains forty new poems, of which all but two appear in translation here.

"Carpet" – Bodil Cappelen, whom Olav H. Hauge married at the age of sixty-nine, is a weaver and painter. When she moved to Ulvik in 1975, Hauge built a workshop for her as an annex to his house.

"Egil" – The poem refers to Egil Skallagrímsson (ca 904–995), whose story is told in *Egil's Saga* (1240). Egil was a Viking warrior, farmer and poet. Some of his poetry, such as *Sonatorrek,* in which he mourns the death of his sons, still survives.

"By the Cabin of Einar Benediktsson" – Einar Benediktsson (1864–1940) was an Icelandic poet whose writings helped nurture a reawakening cultural identity that strongly contributed to Iceland's independence from Denmark in 1918.

"Paul Celan" – Paul Celan (1920–1970) was a German poet. Hauge translated a number of his poems.

"After Reading Guillevic" --Eugène Guillevic (1907–1997) was yet another French poet whom Hauge translated.

"Snow In Castile" – The poem is a homage to Castile and to the Spanish poet Antonio Machado (1875–1939).

"Stare Miasto, Warsaw" – Stare Miasto is the old town of Warsaw. When Hauge visited Poland with his wife in 1986, he was deeply impressed by the beautiful reconstruction that had been done of buildings and monuments damaged or destroyed during World War II. He felt this was an immense contrast to the reconstruction of Nidaros Cathedral in Trondheim, on which construction started in 1869 after twenty-eight years of preparation. It was not completed until 2001, seven years after Hauge's death.

One of the key landmarks in Warsaw is the Sigismund's Column, a nine foot tall bronze statue of King Sigismund III Vasa, perched atop a sixty-three foot tall column in the Castle Square. In 1596 he moved the capital from Kraków to Warsaw. During the Warsaw Uprising in 1944, German forces demolished the column and badly damaged his statue. After the war, the repaired statue of Sigismund was restored to its prominence, raised on a new granite column. Tellingly, the Polish king wields a cross in one hand and a sword in the other.

"Roads" – The first lines of this poem are a quote from *Heiðreksgátur*, a collection of riddles associated with King Heidrek, a major character in the *Tyrfing Cycle*, a Norse myth about a magical sword. This particular riddle describes a bridge!

An interesting bit of trivia: *The Saga of King Heidrek the Wise* was translated by Christopher Tolkien, son of the author of *Lord of the Rings*. Both father and son learned Icelandic in order to read ancient Norse literature in the original.

The Old Norse manuscript *Konungs skuggsjá* (*The King's Mirror*), which was written to educate the future King Magnus VI Law-Mender, describes, among other things, the marvels of faraway lands settled by the Norsemen. It tells of a wondrous Lake Loghica in Ireland, where there is a floating island on which there grow healing herbs – but only one person may come upon it at a time.

"Orvar-Odd" – Orvar-Odd is celebrated in a 13th-century saga written by an unknown author. The legendary hero was a master archer who won many battles. According to the saga, Orvar-Odd (whose name meant "Arrow-Point") traveled far and wide, including to the Mediterranean and the Holy Land. Eventually he returned home.

Arjuna is the hero of the *Bhagavad Gita*, and son of the sky god Indra. On the battlefield, while in a chariot standing between two opposing armies before the fighting begins, Arjuna receives profound lessons on life and the nature of reality from Krishna, disguised as his charioteer. The essence of the teaching is, "Established in Self, perform action" ("*yogastha kuru karmani*", chapter 2.48).

"I Pass the Arctic Circle" – This poem was written after Hauge made his first journey to Northern Norway.

Uncollected poems

"The Cell" – This posthumously published poem refers to Hauge's room or cell at Valen Psychiatric Hospital. All in all, he spent more than five years of his life in the asylum.

Translator's Note

I would like to express my sincere thanks to Bodil Cappelen, wife of Olav H. Hauge, who initiated the creation of this collection of new translations of Hauge's poems, with excerpts from the poet's journals. We had a close and fruitful dialog while this book was evolving. In addition, I am deeply grateful for suggestions and criticism from Hugo Grinebiter; Shelah Horvitz; from Idar Stegane, Professor of Nordic Literature and a renowned Hauge expert; and from my publisher, Dennis Maloney, poet and master translator.

I would also like to express my thanks to Geir Netland and Stein Arnold Hevrøy of the Olav H. Hauge Centre in Ulvik, Norway, for offering their expertise and access to their photographic archives, to Morten Krogvold for permission to reproduce the Hauge portrait used on page fifteen, and to Odd Nerbø for allowing his Hauge photos to be included here. Thanks to Elaine LaMattina for the cover photograph of the poet's home and for her elegant book design.

While I have concentrated on Hauge's free-verse poems, I have also included a number of structured poems. However, in general, I have not tried to recreate Hauge's rhymes. All too often translators who do so tend to perform syntactic contortions, abandoning spoken English and recreating the rhyming structure while sacrificing the very poem itself. Perhaps it is worth mentioning that I have favored the Anglo-Saxon part of the English language, and the surprisingly many English words that are rooted in Old Norse. In my experience, words with Latin and Greek roots, even those arriving indirectly via French or Italian or Spanish, tend to have a more cerebral quality and be less visceral.

When you read Hauge's original Norwegian or listen to recordings of Olav H. Hauge reading his own poems, the sound and music of his language make you feel as though transported to and through the physical landscape itself. The cadence has a quality reminiscent of a chanting Norse bard; Hauge conjures forth situations, and the subject matter of the poem, and makes it truly come alive for the reader.

Like no other poet I know, Olav H. Hauge draws you into his dark and luminous spaces.

Olav Grinde

Olav Grinde has previously published *Night Open: Selected Poems of Rolf Jacobsen* (White Pine Press, Buffalo, 1993). In addition to extensive selections of Olav H. Hauge and Rolf Jacobsen, he has translated Norwegian poets such as Stein Mehren, Marie Takvam, Eldrid Lunden, Hans Børli and Arne Ruste. His translations have appeared in many literary magazines and in numerous anthologies.

He has also translated a variety of museum exhibitions, essays on architecture and other subjects, and books on Norwegian art and music, including *Edvard Grieg – His Life and Music* by Erling Dahl, Jr. Other translated titles include *The Living Sea: Life Along the Norwegian Coast* by Stein Mortensen, and *Northern Passage* by Børge Ousland and Thorleif Thorleifsson.

Olav Grinde is the author of *The Magic of Fjord Norway* , *Cruising Norwegian Waters, Fjord Norway,* and *Turgleder i Hordaland* (Norwegian only).

His chosen challenge is travel writing, translation, professional copywriting, and strategic comunication in a world filled with noise and static. Olav and his wife, Shelah, divide their time between Boston, their homestead in Maine, and Bergen, Norway.

Further Reading – by and about Olav H. Hauge

In English

Robert Bly and Robert Hedin: *The Dream We Carry: Selected and Last Poems of Olav H. Hauge,* Copper Canyon Press, Washington, 2008.

Robin Fulton: *Leaf-Huts and Snow-Houses,* Anvil Press, London, 2003.

Katherine Jane Hansen: *Nature Imagery in Olav H. Hauge's Poetry* (Doctoral dissertation), University of Washington, 1978.

By Olav H. Hauge (in Norwegian)

Dikt i samling, (9th ed.), Oslo, 2010.

Dagbok 1924–1994, (5 volumes), Samlaget, Oslo, 2000.

Dikt i umsetjing, Samlaget, Oslo, 2001.

Frå Rimbaud til Celan: nye dikt i umsetjing, Samlaget, Oslo, 1991.

Mange års røynsle med pil og boge, (book & CD), Samlaget, Oslo, 1988.

ABC, (Bodil Cappelen, illustr.), Samlaget, Oslo, 1986.

Other books in Norwegian

Knut Olav Åmås: *Mitt liv var draum: ein biografi om Olav H. Hauge,* Samlaget, Oslo, 2004.

Bodil Cappelen & Ronny Spaas (ed.): *Tid å hausta inn: 31 forfattarar om Olav H. Hauge*, Samlaget, Oslo, 2008.

Jan Erik Vold: *Under Hauges ord: essays, samtaler, brev, dikt, fotos*, Samlaget, Oslo, 1996.

Jan Erik Vold (ed.): *Syn oss åkeren din*, Bokklubben, Oslo, 1975.

Idar Stegane: *Dikt og artiklar om dikt. Til Olav H. Hauge på 70-årsdagen*, Noregs Boklag, 1978.

Idar Stegane: *Olav H. Hauges dikting*, Noregs Boklag, 1974.

Ole Karlsen: *Streiflys: Om moderne nordisk lyrikk*, Unipubforlag, Oslo, 2006.

In German

Klaus Anders: *Olav H. Hauge: Gesammelte Gedichte*, Edition Rugerup, Berlin, 2012.